Working with an Android 4.4 Tablet for Seniors

Studio Visual Steps

Working with an Android 4.4 Tablet for Seniors

Suitable for tablets from different manufacturers

www.visualsteps.com

This book has been written using the Visual Steps™ method.
Cover design by Studio Willemien Haagsma bNO

© 2015 Visual Steps
Author: Studio Visual Steps

First printing: January 2015
ISBN 978 90 5905 370 0

Resources used: A number of definitions and explanations of computer terminology are taken over from the User Guides of the *Asus tablet*, *Google Nexus tablet* and *Polaroid tablet*.

Do you have questions or suggestions?
E-mail: info@visualsteps.com

Would you like more information?
www.visualsteps.com

Website for this book:
www.visualsteps.com/tablet44

Subscribe to the free Visual Steps Newsletter:
www.visualsteps.com/newsletter

Table of Contents

Foreword

Tablets have become an integral part of our society. The range of tablets available on the market these days has grown explosively in the past few years. The developments in the field of tablet design are rapidly increasing as well. Even tablets in the lower price ranges are steadily improving.

There are many companies that make and market tablets. The most popular operating system used on tablets today is the *Android* operating system. In general, all tablets running *Android*, from version 4.0 and higher, function in much the same way. Some manufacturers however will brand or customize their devices by adapting the home screen design and offering a combination of open source and proprietary software. Still the basic operation of an *Android* tablet and the way in which the apps work are for the most part very similar.

This book covers the basic operations for using an *Android 4.4* tablet in an easy, step by step manner. Popular tasks that can be done on a tablet such as sending and receiving email, surfing the Internet, getting directions, and keeping a calendar are thoroughly explained. Usually an *Android* tablet will contain one or more standard apps (programs) that allow you to view photos, watch videos, and play music. There are chapters in this book that will help you get acquainted with these apps. You can search the *Play Store* for additional free and paid apps that allow you to accomplish many other tasks and activities. For example, there are apps for games, puzzles, newspapers and even photo editing. With this book you will learn how to work with the most commonly used functions, options and settings on a tablet running the *Android 4.4* operating system (also known as *KitKat*).

I hope you have a lot of fun learning to work with your tablet!

Emma Schipper
Studio Visual Steps

PS We welcome your comments and suggestions.
Our email address is: info@visualsteps.com

Newsletter

All Visual Steps books follow the same methodology: clear and concise step-by-step instructions with screenshots to demonstrate each task.
A complete list of all our books can be found on our website **www.visualsteps.com**
You can also sign up to receive our **free Visual Steps Newsletter** by email.
In this Newsletter you will receive periodic information by email regarding:
- the latest titles and previously released books;
- special offers, supplemental chapters, tips and free informative booklets.

Our Newsletter subscribers may also download the free informative guides and booklets listed on the web page **www.visualsteps.com/info_downloads**

Introduction to Visual Steps™

The Visual Steps books are the best instructional materials available for learning how to work with mobile devices, computers and software applications. Nowhere else will you find better support for getting started with *Windows*, *Mac OS X*, an iPad or other tablet, an iPhone, or various software applications such as *Picasa*.

Characteristics of the Visual Steps books:
- **Comprehensible contents**
  Addresses the needs of the beginner or intermediate computer user for a manual written in simple, straight-forward language.
- **Clear structure**
  Precise, easy to follow instructions. The material is broken down into small enough segments to allow for easy absorption.
- **Screenshots of every step**
  Quickly compare what you see on your screen with the screenshots in the book. Pointers and tips guide you when new windows are opened so you always know what to do next.
- **Get started right away**
  All you have to do is turn on your device and have your book at hand. Perform each operation as indicated on your own device.
- **Layout**
  The text is printed in a large size font and is clearly legible.

In short, I believe these manuals will be excellent guides for you.

Dr. H. van der Meij
Faculty of Applied Education, Department of Instructional Technology, University of Twente, the Netherlands

What You Will Need

In order to work through this book, you will need a number of things:

A tablet with *Android 4.4* installed.

The screens you see on your own tablet may look different from the images in this book. The buttons may also have a different name and/or look a little different. Always try to find a similar button or function. The basic operations will remain the same.

It is also useful to have one of the following devices nearby.

A computer or laptop for transferring photos, video, and music. If you do not own a computer or laptop, you can just skip the actions where these are mentioned.

How to Use This Book

This book has been written using the Visual Steps™ method. The method is simple: place the book on a surface where you can easily read it. Hold you *Android* tablet and perform each task as described, step by step, directly on your own tablet. With the clear instructions and the multitude of screenshots, you will always know exactly what to do next. By working through all the tasks in each chapter, you will gain a full understanding of your *Android* tablet. You can also skip a chapter and go to one which best suits your needs.

In this Visual Steps™ book, you will see various icons. This is what they mean:

Techniques:
These icons indicate an action to be carried out:

The index finger indicates that you need to do something on the tablet's screen, for example, tap something.

The keyboard icon means you should type something on the keyboard of your tablet or computer.

The mouse icon means you need to do something on your computer by using the mouse.

The hand icon means you should do something else, for example, rotate the tablet, or turn it off. It can also point to a task previously learned.

In some areas of this book additional icons indicate warnings or helpful hints. These may help you avoid common mistakes and will alert you when a decision needs to be made.

Help
These icons indicate that extra help is available:

 The arrow icon warns you about something.

 The bandage icon will help you if something has gone wrong.

 Have you forgotten how to do something? The number next to the footsteps tells you where to look it up at the end of the book, in the appendix *How Do I Do That Again?*

In separate boxes you will find tips or additional background information.

Extra information
Information boxes are denoted by these icons:

 The book icon gives you extra background information that you can read at your convenience. This extra information is not necessary for working through the book.

The light bulb icon indicates an extra tip for using the tablet.

Website

This book is accompanied by a website, **www.visualsteps.com/tablet44**
Be sure to visit this website from time to time, to see if we have added any additional information, supplemental chapters or errata for this book.

For Teachers

The Visual Steps books have been written as self-study guides for individual use. They are also well suited for use in a group or a classroom setting. For this purpose, some of our books come with a free teacher's manual. You can download the available teacher's manuals and additional materials from the website:
www.visualsteps.com/instructor

The Screenshots

The screenshots in this book indicate which button, file, or hyperlink you need to tap in your screen. In the instruction text (in **bold** letters) you will see a small image of the item you need to click. The line will point you to the right place on your screen.

The small screenshots that are printed in this book are not meant to be completely legible all the time. This is not necessary, as you will see these images on your own screen in real size and fully legible.

Here you see an example of an instruction text and a screenshot of the item you need to tap. The line indicates where to find this item on your own screen:

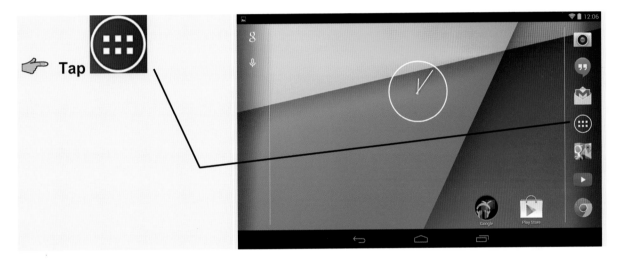

Sometimes the screenshot shows only a portion of a window. Here is an example:

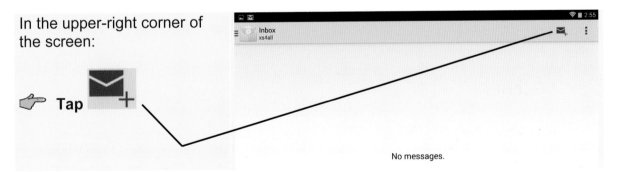

We would like to emphasize that we **do not intend yo**u read all the information in the screenshots in this book. Always use the screenshots in combination with the larger display on the screen of your tablet.

1. Getting Started with Your Tablet

You can do many different things with your tablet. Not just surfing the Internet and emailing, but also maintaining a calendar, playing games, listening to music, watching videos, and reading books, newspapers, and magazines. All these things are done by using *apps*. These are the programs that are installed on the tablet. In addition to the standard apps, you can add more apps (both free and paid) using the web store for apps called *Play Store*.

You can connect to the Internet on your tablet through a wireless network (Wi-Fi). Wi-Fi provides access to the Internet over a distance of roughly 100 meters (328 feet). This access will depend on the router and the environment in which you are using the tablet. Sometimes there are public connections where you can use Wi-Fi right away, but usually the Wi-Fi connection is secured with a password.

Some tablets can connect to the Internet through a 3G/4G mobile data network. This type of connection is useful in places where no Wi-Fi is available, but it does require a 3G/4G data subscription or a prepaid SIM card. Ask your telecom provider for options available for your tablet.

In this chapter you will get to know your tablet and learn the basic operations for using it.

In this chapter you will learn how to:

- turn on or unlock your tablet;
- set up your tablet;
- recognize the main components of a tablet;
- perform basic operations on the tablet;
- connect to the Internet through Wi-Fi;
- connect to the Internet through a mobile data network;
- create and add a *Google* account;
- update your tablet;
- lock or turn off your tablet.

➥ Please note:

Tablets running the *Android 4.4* operating system will all work roughly in the same way. Sometimes, the home screen looks a little different and the buttons are located in a different spot. This means the images in this book may not completely match the screens on your tablet. But this does not really matter, as the basic operations you will be learning about in this book are identical.

1.1 Turning On or Unlocking Your Tablet

➥ Please note:

For the most part, the screenshots in this book have been made while holding the tablet in what is called 'landscape mode'. This means holding the tablet with the longer side placed horizontally. We recommend holding the tablet in this position while you work through this book.

Your tablet may be turned off or locked. This is how you turn on your tablet, in case it has been turned off:

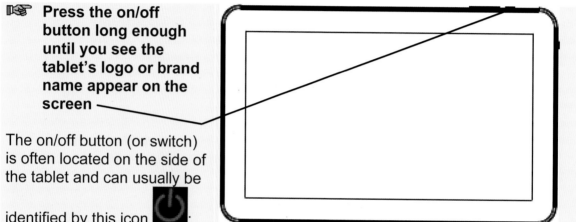

☞ **Press the on/off button long enough until you see the tablet's logo or brand name appear on the screen**

The on/off button (or switch) is often located on the side of the tablet and can usually be

identified by this icon ⏻ :

Source: User manual Polaroid tablet

The tablet will be turned on.

The tablet may also be locked. The screen will be dark and will not react to touch gestures. If this is the case, you can unlock the tablet like this:

☞ **Briefly press the on/off button**

If you have previously used your tablet, you will probably need to unlock the screen in the following manner:

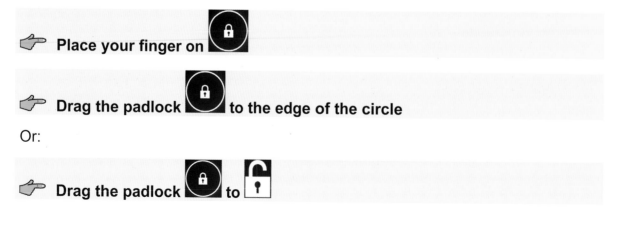

☞ **Place your finger on** 🔒

☞ **Drag the padlock** 🔒 **to the edge of the circle**

Or:

☞ **Drag the padlock** 🔒 **to** 🔓

If you are starting up your tablet for the first time, you will see a few screens where you need to enter basic information to set up your tablet. In the next section you can read how to do this. If you have used your tablet before, you can continue on page 25 with *section 1.3 The Main Components of a Tablet.*

1.2 Setting Up the Tablet

You can choose the language for the tablet:

🔖 Please note:

The screens on your own tablet may look different from the images in this book. The buttons may also have a different name and/or look different. Always look for a similar button or function. The basic operations will always remain the same.

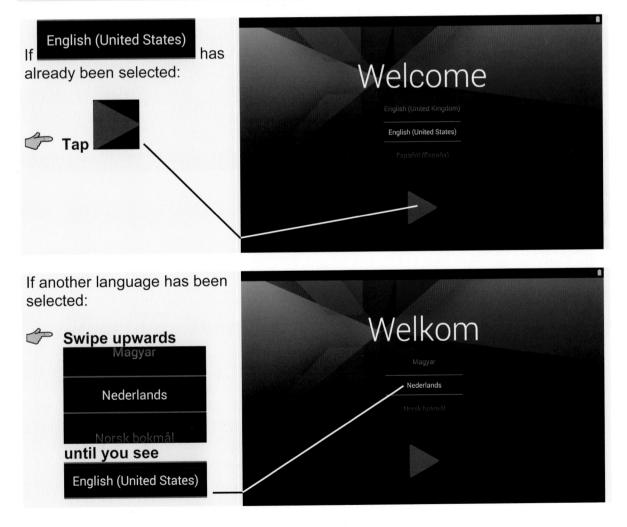

If English (United States) has already been selected:

☞ **Tap**

If another language has been selected:

☞ **Swipe upwards**

Magyar

Nederlands

Norsk bokmål

until you see

English (United States)

👉 **Tap**

If you are within range of a Wi-Fi network, you can select this network.

If the network is secured, you will see a small padlock 🔒 next to the name of the network. In that case you will need to enter a password:

👉 **Tap the desired Wi-Fi-network**

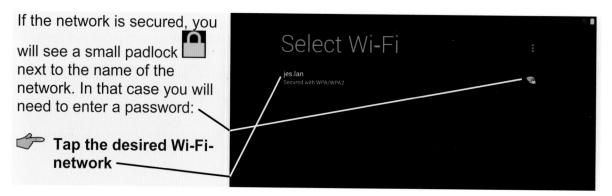

🐾 **Please note:**

If you use an unsecured, public Wi-Fi connection, be aware of the risks this may entail. In the *Background information* at the end of this chapter you will find a number of tips about safeguarding sensitive information.

You only need to perform the following action if it is a secure Wi-Fi network:

⌨ **If necessary, type the password**

👉 **If necessary, tap** **Connect**

A connection is established with the Wi-Fi network.

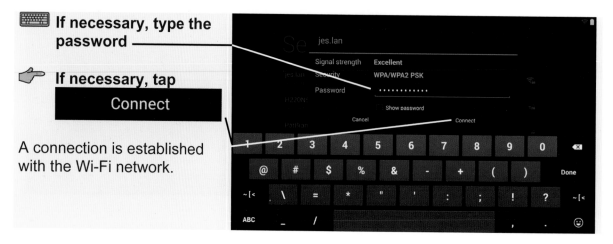

♡ Tip

Typing on a tablet

You can type on a tablet by tapping the letters.

To type a capital letter, tap

To type numbers, tap

To return to the keyboard with the letters, tap

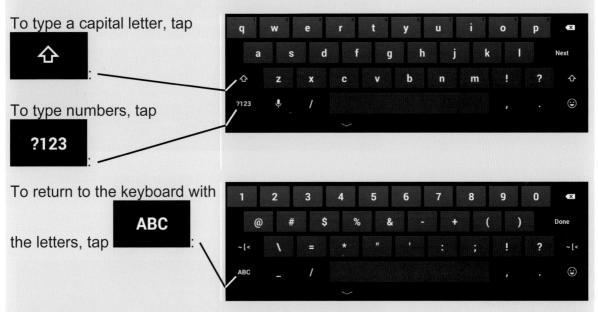

In *Chapter 2 Using Email on Your Tablet* you will find more information about typing on your tablet.

In the next screen you will be asked for your *Google* account. Many *Google* and *Android* functions require you to have a *Google* account. A *Google* account is a combination of an email address and a password. For now, you can skip this step. You can read how to create a *Google* account later on in this chapter in *section 1.7 Creating and Adding a Google account*.

☞ **Tap**

☞ **Tap**

In the next screen you will be asked whether you want to use the *Google location services*. This function uses Wi-Fi data to determine your physical location, even if you are not using your tablet. It is also used by *Google* to yield applicable search results for your area, for example. If you do not want this:

☞ **If desired, uncheck the boxes** ✔

☞ **Tap**

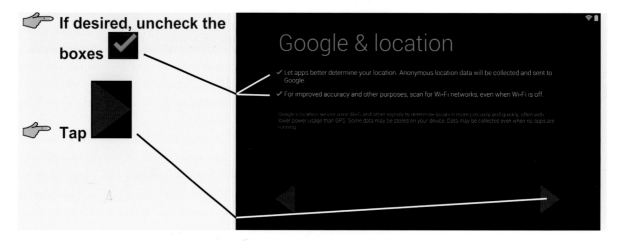

In the next screen you enter the name of the tablet's owner:

⌨ **Type your first name**

☞ **Tap**

Next

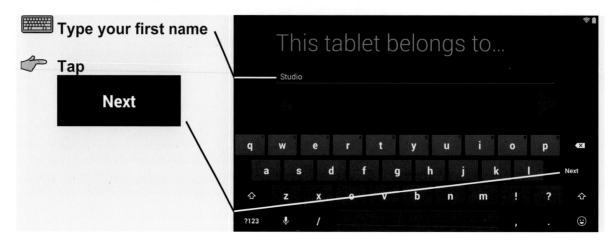

⌨ **Type your last name**

☞ **Tap** ▶

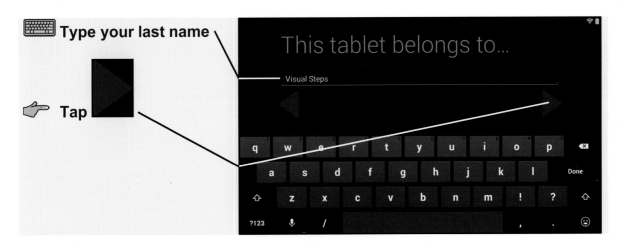

In the following screen you will see a message regarding *Google* services. In order to agree to the terms:

☞ **Tap** ▶

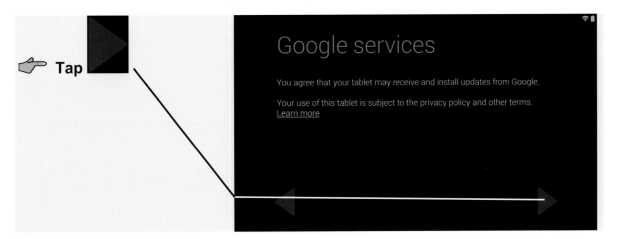

Now the tablet has been set up and is ready to use:

☞ **Tap** ▶ or Finish

You will see the home screen:

☞ **If necessary, tap**

OK

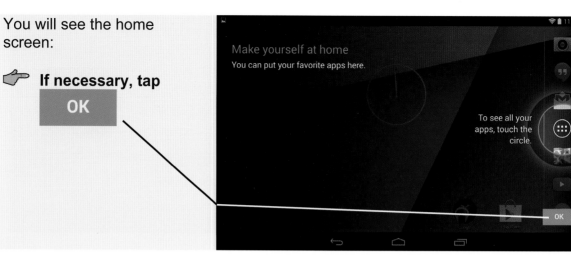

🩹 HELP! My tablet is locked.

If you do not use the tablet for a while, it may lock automatically. This will happen by default, after a set number of minutes. This is how you unlock the tablet:

☞ **Briefly press the on/off button**

☞ **Place your finger on** 🔒

☞ **Drag the padlock** 🔒 **to the edge of the circle**

Or:

☞ **Drag the padlock** 🔒 **to** 🔓

1.3 The Main Components of a Tablet

In the image below you will see a drawing of a tablet showing the main components. Your own tablet may look a bit different, but for the most part the components will be similar. If you wish you can read the manual that goes with your tablet.

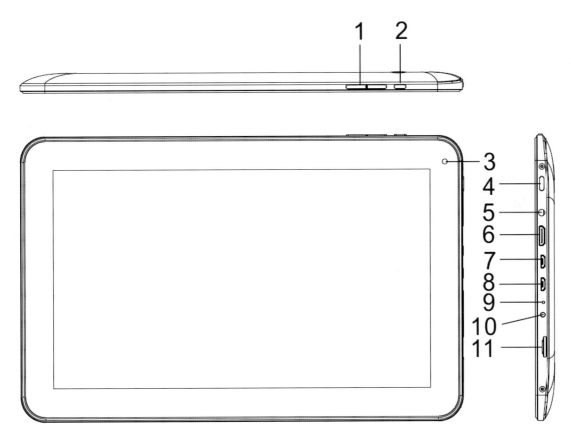

1. Volume control buttons
2. Button to go back to the previous screen
3. Camera on front side of the tablet
4. On/off button
5. Audio output (headphone jack)
6. HDMI port for a TV or other type of monitor
7. USB port
8. USB port for another device or computer
9. Reset button
10. Adapter port (charging adapter)
11. SD card slot

Source: User manual Polaroid tablet

Other components not shown in the image above may be present on your tablet. These might be:
- a SIM card slot;
- a camera on the rear side of the tablet.

If you have a tablet that is suited for both Wi-Fi and a mobile data network (3G/4G), you can place the SIM card that goes with the data subscription (or a prepaid card) in the SIM card slot. If there is a camera on the rear of the tablet, you will be able to take pictures and record videos.

The home screens of various *Android 4.4* tablets may differ from one another. Certain items may be placed in a different spot, or look a little different. The standard set of apps that are installed are not always the same either. But the basic principle will always remain the same.

This is what the home screen of your tablet will look like, more or less:

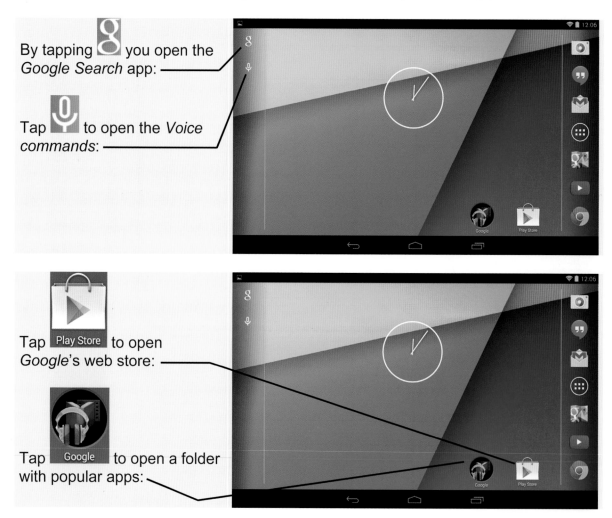

By tapping [g] you open the *Google Search* app: —

Tap [🎤] to open the *Voice commands*: —

Tap [Play Store] to open *Google*'s web store: —

Tap [Google] to open a folder with popular apps: —

On the right side or at the bottom of the screen you see the favorites tray:

The apps in the favorites tray will always remain visible even if you go to another page on your home screen.

Tap to see an overview of all the apps installed on your tablet: ———

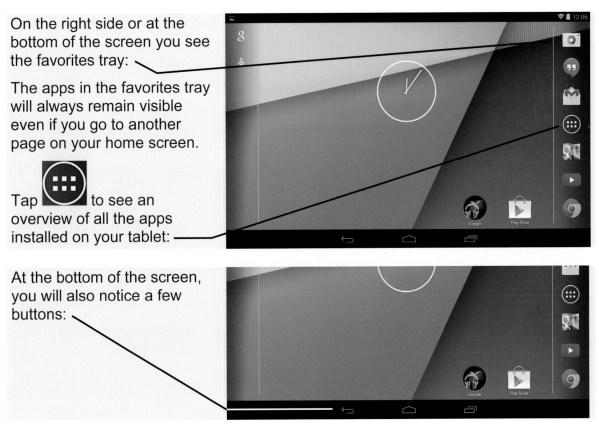

At the bottom of the screen, you will also notice a few buttons:

Here is what you can do with these buttons:

Tap this button to go back to the previous screen.

Tap this button to go to the home screen.

Tap this button to open a list of recently used apps.

➥ Please note:

These buttons may look different on your own tablet, and/or the buttons may be located on a different spot of the screen. You may also have more or fewer buttons on your screen. Examples of other buttons are ▣ and ▣ to turn the volume down or up, ▣ for making screenshots, and ▣ to open the *Quick Settings* window.

💡 Tip

Adjust the volume of the system sounds

If you tap 🔊 or 🔊 (or have pressed one of the volume control buttons), you can also adjust the system sounds on your tablet:

You will see the volume bar:

👉 **Tap** ⚏

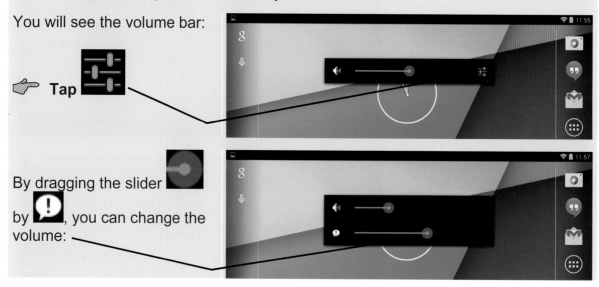

By dragging the slider ⚫

by ❗, you can change the volume:

In the upper-right corner of the screen (next to the time indicator) you will see the system icons. These icons provide information about the status of the tablet and its connections.

📶 indicates the strength of the Wi-Fi connection:

🔋 indicates the battery level:

If you see a thunderbolt ⚡, the tablet is being charged.

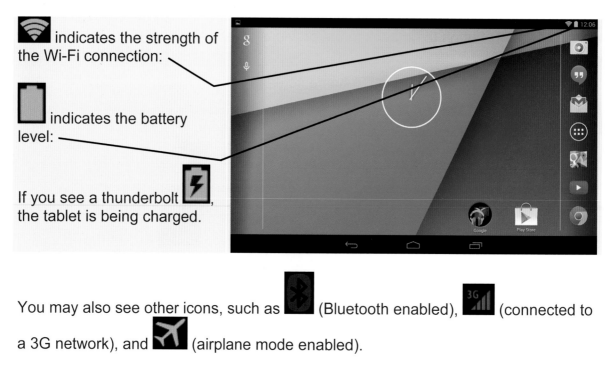

You may also see other icons, such as 🔵 (Bluetooth enabled), 📶 (connected to a 3G network), and ✈ (airplane mode enabled).

1.4 Basic Operations on Your Tablet

Your tablet is easy to use. In this section you will practice some basic operations and touch gestures. If necessary, unlock the tablet first:

☞ **Unlock the tablet** ✇¹

You will see the home screen. Open the *Quick Settings* window:

☞ **Drag downwards from the top right-hand corner of the screen**

The *Quick Settings* window appears:

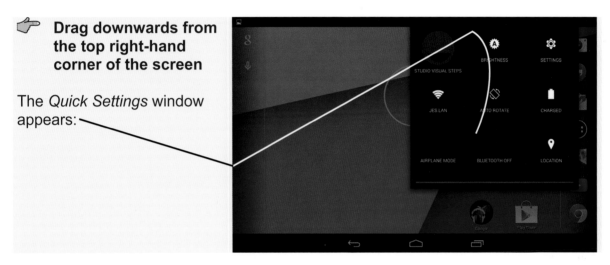

➥ **Please note:**

Depending on the type of tablet you have, the *Quick Settings* window may be located in a different spot, for example, in the middle or top of the screen. The window may also look different.

In this window you can quickly change a few settings.

For instance, you can set the screen to remain in the same position when you turn the tablet to its side:

☞ **Tap** AUTO ROTATE

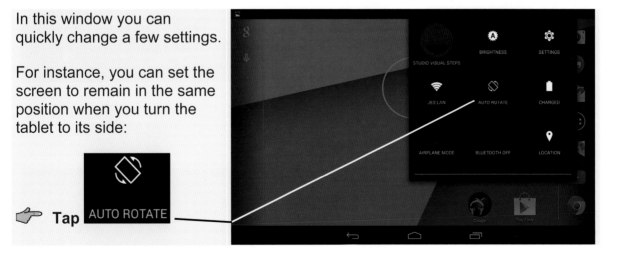

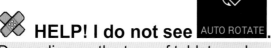 **HELP! I do not see** AUTO ROTATE.

Depending on the type of tablet you have, you may not see this button. In that case, you can try this:

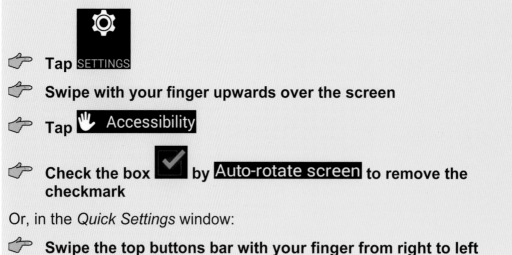

☞ **Tap** SETTINGS

☞ **Swipe with your finger upwards over the screen**

☞ **Tap** 🖐 **Accessibility**

☞ **Check the box** ✔️ **by** Auto-rotate screen **to remove the checkmark**

Or, in the *Quick Settings* window:

☞ **Swipe the top buttons bar with your finger from right to left**

Now you can check to see if this works:

☞ **Hold the tablet in an upright (vertical) position**

You will see that the image on the tablet will not rotate along with the tablet. It has been locked in landscape (horizontal) mode. If you do want the image on the tablet to rotate, you can do this:

☞ **Tap** ROTATION LOCKED

You can use the *Quick Settings* window to open the *Settings* app. On the *Settings* app you can adjust a large number of settings for your tablet, such as the sound settings, the view, and the security settings.

To open the *Settings* app:

☞ **Tap** SETTINGS

💡 Tip

Another way to open the *Settings* app

You can also open the *Settings* app in this way:

☞ **If necessary, tap**

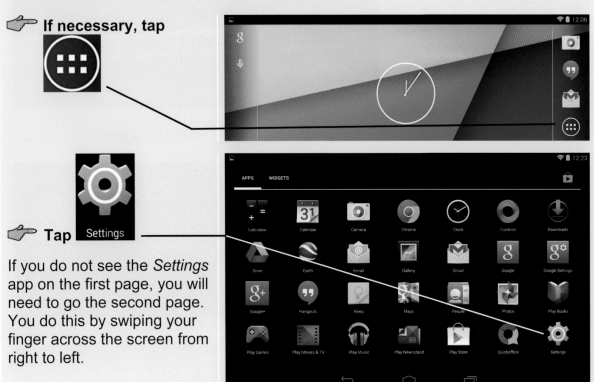

☞ **Tap** Settings

If you do not see the *Settings* app on the first page, you will need to go the second page. You do this by swiping your finger across the screen from right to left.

The *Settings* app contains many more items than can be displayed on the screen at one time. To view the rest of the list:

☞ **Drag with you finger upwards over the screen**

This type of touch gesture is called scrolling. In *section 3.4 Scrolling* you will read more about this gesture.

You can also scroll the other way:

☞ **Drag with your finger downwards over the screen**

You will see the beginning of the list again:

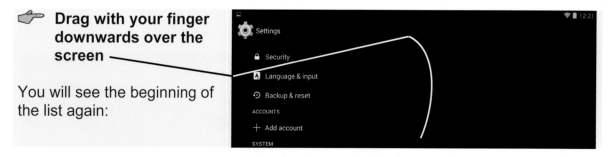

This is how you quit the *Settings* app and go back to the home screen:

☞ **Tap**

Depending on the type of tablet you have, you may see a slightly different button, for example ![house icon].

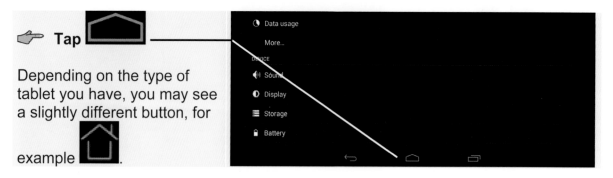

1.5 Connecting to the Internet through Wi-Fi

Your tablet will always connect automatically to the Wi-Fi network it was previously connected to. You can connect to a different Wi-Fi network manually if you want to use your tablet somewhere else, for example, at a friend's or at a hotel or restaurant. Of course, this will only be possible if there is a Wi-Fi network available. If a password is required (for a secured network), you will need to ask for it.

➥ **Please note:**

In order to do the following steps, you will need to have access to another Wi-Fi network. If you do not have one available, you can just read through this section.

You connect to another Wi-Fi network through the *Quick Access* window:

☞ **Drag downwards, from the top right-hand corner of the screen**

☞ **Tap**

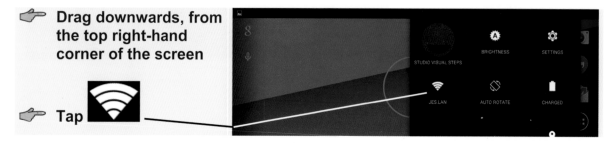

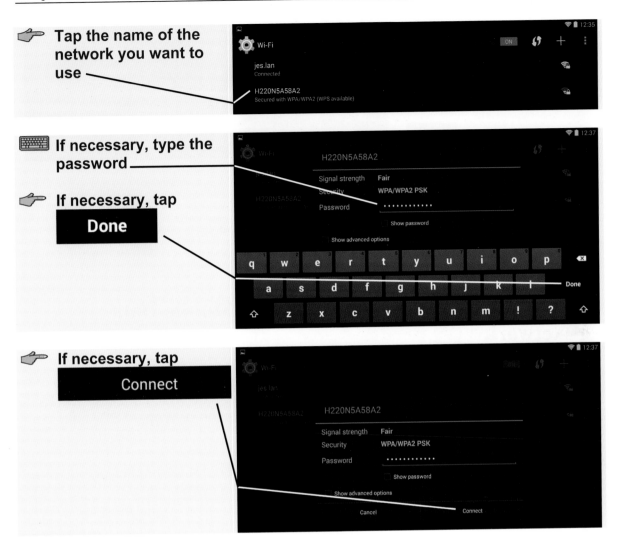

👉 **Tap the name of the network you want to use**

⌨ **If necessary, type the password**

👉 **If necessary, tap**

Done

👉 **If necessary, tap**

Connect

You will be connected to the wireless network.

👉 **Go to the home screen** 👣²

If you want to disable this Wi-Fi connection:

👉 **Open the *Settings* app** 👣³

👉 **Tap** ON

The button turns into OFF :

The Wi-Fi connection is no longer active.

To enable the Wi-Fi
connection again:

☞ **Tap** OFF

The button turns into ON :

☞ **Go to the home screen** 👣²

The next time your tablet is within range of this Wi-Fi network, it will connect
automatically to it.

1.6 Connecting to the Internet with a Mobile Data Network

When you are traveling and cannot access a Wi-Fi network, you may still want to use
the Internet. Some tablets are equipped with a SIM card slot, which enables you to
use a mobile data network (3G/4G) with a data subscription or prepaid SIM card from
a telecom provider.

There are different types of SIM cards. It depends on your tablet which type you need
to use.

👉 **Please note:**
Ask your telecom provider for the options available regarding the use of a mobile
Internet connection on your tablet.

Before you insert the SIM card, be sure to completely turn off the tablet:

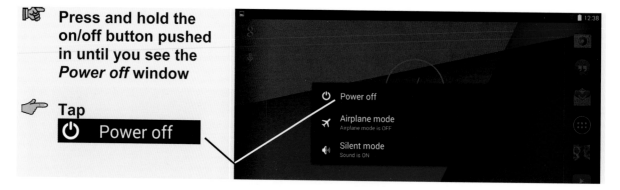

☞ **Press and hold the
on/off button pushed
in until you see the
Power off window**

☞ **Tap**
⏻ **Power off**

You will be asked if you really want to turn off the tablet:

☞ **Tap** **OK**

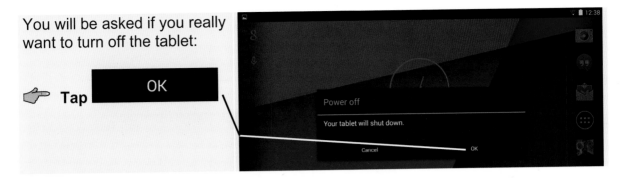

The way in which you open the SIM card slot can differ per tablet. Consult your tablet's manual to find out how to do this.

☞ **Open the SIM card slot**

☞ **Insert the SIM card into the SIM card slot**

☞ **Continue to push it gently in until the SIM card clicks in place**

Make sure not to touch the gold-colored part. This could damage the SIM card.

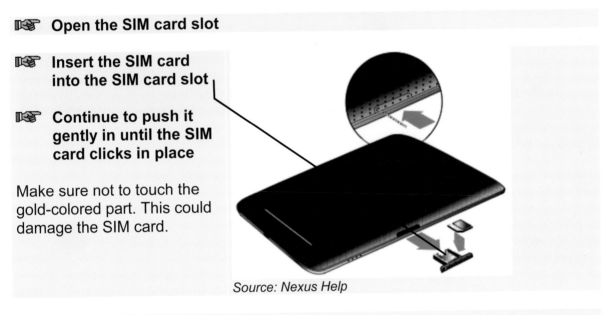

Source: Nexus Help

☞ **Close the SIM card slot**

☞ **Turn on the tablet again** 👣[1]

You will connect automatically to the mobile data network. As soon as the connection has been established, you will see a new system icon appear 📶 in the upper-right corner of the screen.

➥**Please note:**
If you are not automatically connected, you may need to adjust some of the settings. Ask your telecom provider for the correct settings.

If you want to temporarily disable the Internet connection through a mobile data network, you do that like this:

☞ **Open the *Settings* app** ✍³

👉 Tap More...

👉 Tap **Mobile networks**

👉 **Uncheck the box** ☑ by **Data roaming**

You can activate the mobile network connection again by checking the box ☑ by **Data roaming**.

➘ **Please note:**

If you are using mobile data, the **Data roaming** function is disabled by default. *Data roaming* means that you can use the data network of a different telecom provider, in the case that you cannot connect to your own provider's network. Be careful when enabling data roaming however, especially if you are travelling abroad. It can lead to very high data roaming costs.

☞ **Go to the home screen** ✍²

1.7 Creating and Adding a Google Account

Many *Google* and *Android* functions require a *Google* account. A *Google* account is a combination of an email address and a password. In this section you are going to create a new *Google* account. If you already have a *Google* account you can use that.

☞ **Unlock the tablet** 🐾^{1}

☞ **Open the *Settings* app** 🐾^{3}

👆 **Swipe upwards over the screen**

👆 **Tap** ➕ **Add account**

👈 **Tap** 8⃣ **Google**

If you already have a *Google* account:

👆 **Tap** **Existing**

⌨ **Type the data**

☞ **Follow the instructions in the next few screens and continue with *section 1.8 Manually Updating Your Tablet***

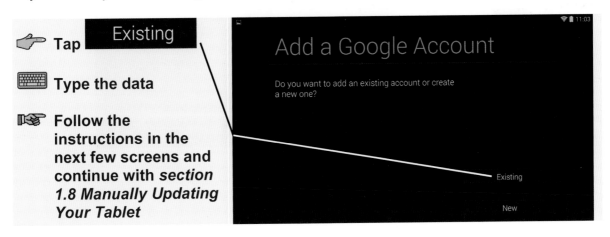

In order to create a new *Google* account:

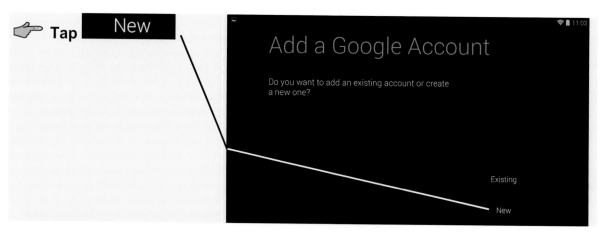

When you are entering the data for your *Google* account, it is easier if you hold the tablet upright (in a vertical position). If you hold the tablet in a horizontal (landscape) position, you will need to scroll more to see the other fields on the screen.

☞ Hold the tablet upright (in a vertical position)

First, you enter your first and last name:

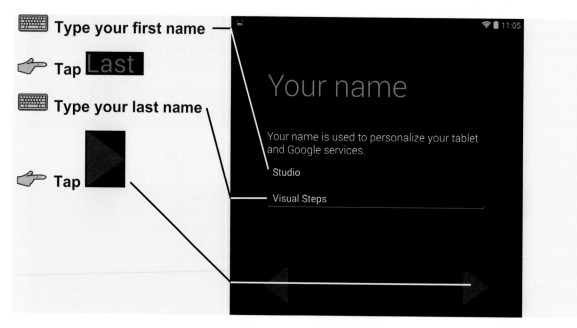

You can create your own email address. This email address ends in @gmail.com.

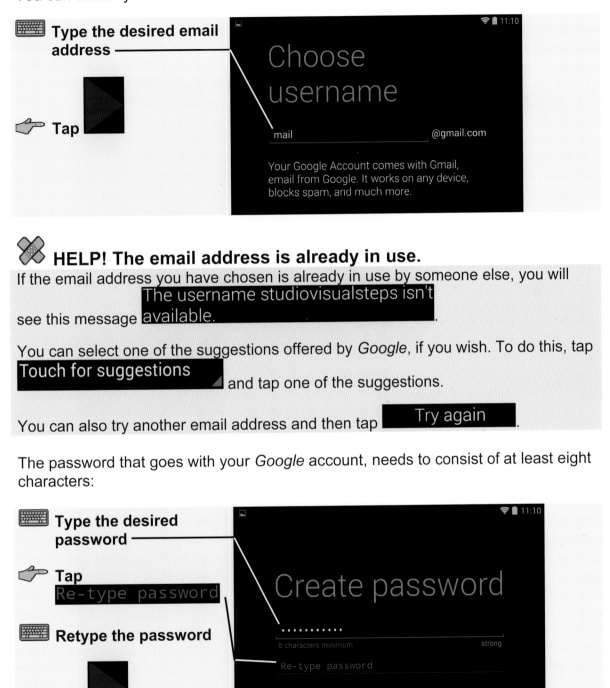

Type the desired email address

Tap

Choose username

mail   @gmail.com

Your Google Account comes with Gmail, email from Google. It works on any device, blocks spam, and much more.

HELP! The email address is already in use.

If the email address you have chosen is already in use by someone else, you will see this message The username studiovisualsteps isn't available.

You can select one of the suggestions offered by *Google*, if you wish. To do this, tap Touch for suggestions and tap one of the suggestions.

You can also try another email address and then tap Try again.

The password that goes with your *Google* account, needs to consist of at least eight characters:

Type the desired password

Tap Re-type password

Retype the password

Tap

Create password

••••••••••
8 characters minimum   strong

Re-type password

You will now be given the option of setting up recovery options by entering your mobile telephone number and/or other email adresss. With this information, *Google* can check whether you are actually the person who is allowed to ask for the password in case you happen to forget it in the future:

☞ **Tap**
Set up recovery options

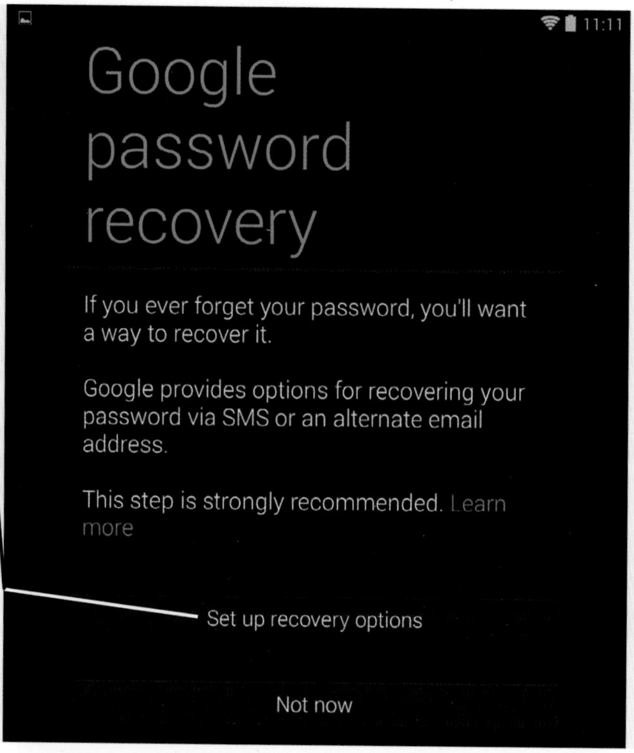

☞ **If desired, type the mobile telephone number**

And/or:

☞ **Tap** Backup email

☞ **If desired, type an alternative email address**

☞ **Tap** ▶

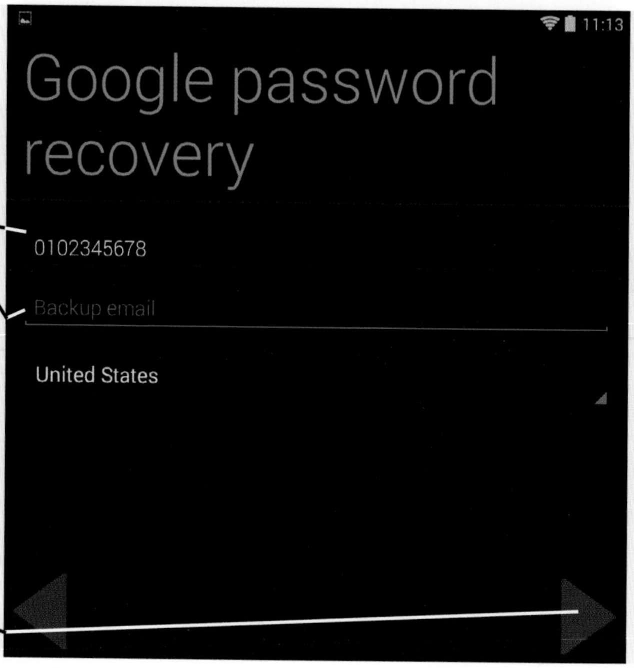

A backup of your data and settings is made by default to your *Google* account. If you do not want this to happen, you can uncheck this option. If you want to be kept informed of the latest news and offers from *Google Play,* check the option by Communication.

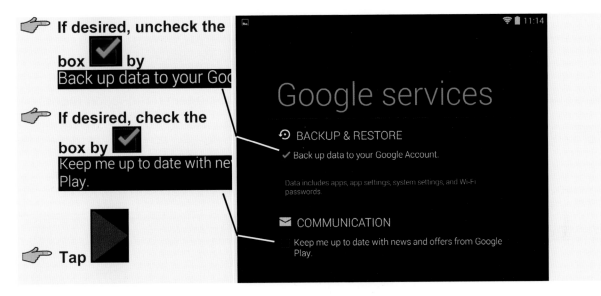

If desired, uncheck the box ✔ **by** Back up data to your Goo

If desired, check the box by ✔ Keep me up to date with ne Play.

Tap ▶

In order to continue you will need to agree to *Google's* servicing terms and privacy policy:

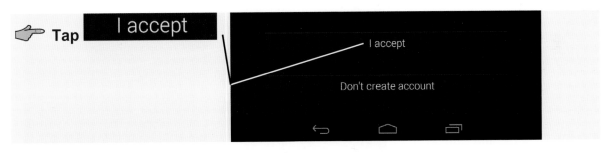

Tap I accept

You will see a box with some characters you need to type for verification:

Type the text you see in the white box —

At the bottom of the screen:

Tap ▶

You will be connected to *Google* and your account will be saved:

Now you can turn the tablet back to the horizontal position again (landscape mode).

☞ **Hold the tablet in the horizontal position**

You will be asked if you want to use *Google+*. This is *Google's* version of a social network site comparable to websites such as *Facebook*. You can skip this for now:

☞ **Tap** Not now

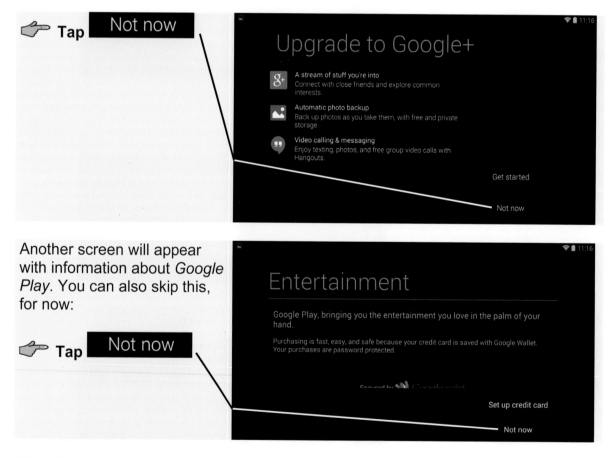

Another screen will appear with information about *Google Play*. You can also skip this, for now:

☞ **Tap** Not now

Your *Google* account has been added to your tablet:

☞ **Go to the home screen** 𝒶𝒶²

1.8 Manually Updating Your Tablet

If new software becomes available for your tablet, you will usually receive a message about that right away. Some tablets also have a function with which you can check for updates manually, and then install them.

This is how you can manually check for new available updates:

☞ **Unlock the tablet** 𝒫[1]

☞ **Open the *Settings* app** 𝒫[3]

☞ **Swipe downwards over the screen**

☞ **Tap ⓘ About tablet**

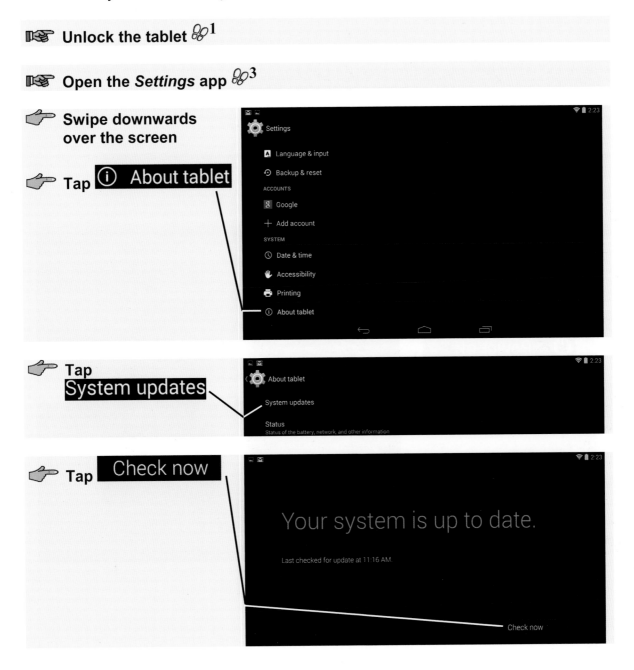

☞ **Tap System updates**

☞ **Tap Check now**

If new software is available, you can now install it.

☞ **If necessary, follow the instructions in the next few screens**

☞ **Go to the home screen** 👣²

1.9 Locking or Turning Off Your Tablet

If you stop working on your tablet, you can either lock it or turn it off completely. If you lock it, the tablet will still be turned on, but consume less power. If you have disabled Wi-Fi, the tablet will hardly use any power at all. This is how you lock the tablet:

☞ **Briefly press the on/off button**

The screen will turn off and no longer react to touch gestures.

If you want to completely turn off the tablet, this is how you do it:

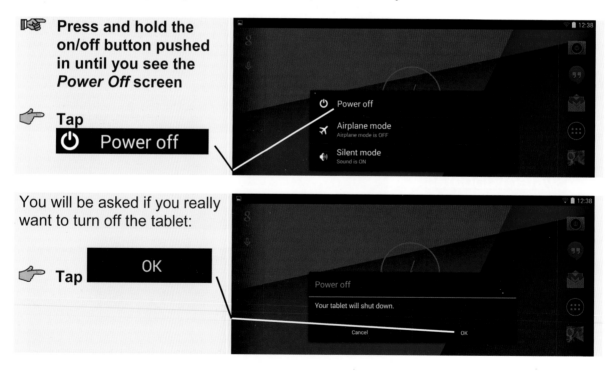

☞ **Press and hold the on/off button pushed in until you see the *Power Off* screen**

☞ **Tap**
 ⏻ **Power off**

You will be asked if you really want to turn off the tablet:

☞ **Tap** **OK**

In the future, you can choose whether to lock or turn off the tablet.

In this chapter you have been introduced to a number of basic operations for using your tablet. You can read some additional information in the *Background Information* and *Tips* sections of this chapter.

1.10 Background Information

Dictionary

Airplane mode	If you have set your tablet to this mode, you cannot access the Internet and you cannot use any Bluetooth devices.
Android	An operating system for mobile phones (smartphones), tablets, and other devices. *Android* is not tied to a single, specific manufacturer. *Google* offers *Android* free under open-source licenses to manufacturers of mobile devices. Many of these manufacturers brand their devices with their own unique user interface. The tablets that have been produced all look a little bit different and function in a slightly different way, even though they run the same version of *Android*.
App	Short for application, a program for the tablet.
Bluetooth	An open standard for wireless connections between devices over short distances. For example, you can use Bluetooth to connect a wireless keyboard or a headset to your tablet. Not all tablets are equipped for Bluetooth.
Favorites tray	On the home screen you will find the favorites tray. This function enables you to quickly navigate to your apps, music, et cetera.
Google account	A combination of a user name (email address) and a password, that provides access to *Google* and *Android* functions and services.
Home screen	The screen that appears when you turn on or unlock your tablet.
Lock	You can lock the tablet if you no longer want to use it by disabling the screen with the on/off button. If you touch the screen when the tablet is locked, nothing will happen.
Lock screen	The screen that appears when you turn on the tablet from the locked mode. You need to unlock the lock screen before you can use the tablet.
On/off button	The (power) button with which you can lock, unlock, and turn your tablet on or off.
Play Store	An online store where you can download free and paid apps.
SIM card	SIM stands for *Subscriber Identity Module*. The SIM card is the (small) chip card your telecom provider gives you. You usually need to insert it into your tablet or mobile phone yourself.

Sleep mode	A function that locks the tablet by default after a set number of seconds of not being used.
Tablet, tablet PC	A tablet is a computer without a casing and separate keyboard that can be fully operated by a touch screen.
Wi-Fi	A wireless network for the Internet.
3G	The third generation of standards and technology for mobile phones and tablets. Because of the higher speed, 3G offers more options than previous standards. With 3G you can make phone calls over the Internet, among other things.
4G	4G is the fourth generation of standards and technology for mobile phones and tablets and is even faster than 3G. With 4G you can make phone calls over the Internet, among other things.

Source: User manual Polaroid tablet, Wikipedia

The Android operating system

Android is a mobile operating system for mobile phones (smartphones), tablets, and other devices. It was developed by Android Inc., a company that was taken over by *Google* in 2005. *Android* is not tied to a single specific manufacturer, as is the case with the *iOS* operating system from *Apple*. *Google* offers *Android* free under open-source licenses to various manufacturers of mobile devices.

New *Android* updates are released all the time. In the development stage, the new versions often acquire a code name. The first letters of these code names are placed in alphabetical order:

- 1.5 Cupcake;
- 1.6 Donut;
- 2.0/2.1 Eclair;
- 2.2 Frozen Yoghurt /FroYo;
- 2.3 Gingerbread;
- 3.1/3.2 Honeycomb;
- 4.0 Ice Cream Sandwich;
- 4.1/4.2/4.3 Jelly Bean;
- 4.4 Kit Kat.

A number of smartphone and tablet manufacturers do not use the standard *Android* interface on their devices. This is why tablets from different manufacturers look different and function slightly different from one another even though they run the same version of *Android*.

Public Wi-Fi networks

A public Wi-Fi network is one that anyone can connect to. Sometimes, public networks do not even require a user name or password to establish a connection. If you want to use a public network be aware of the risks involved and avoid sharing sensitive information over the Internet.

Here are a few tips for using a public Wi-Fi network safely:

- **Verify the name of the Wi-Fi network before you connect.**
  Check the name of the network with the staff or on signage before you connect to it. This may help you from connecting to a bogus network set up by cybercriminals, where anything can happen, from the hijacking of your session data to the stealing of sensitive information. Network names can appear very simlar to one another with just one letter being the difference with an untrusted, fraudulent one.

- **Do not sign on automatically with public Wi-Fi networks.**
  If you connect to a particular Wi-Fi network with your tablet, it will automatically connect again if the connection becomes available. You can avoid this by tapping the network name and then tapping the option 'Forget'.

- **Is the Wi-Fi network secured with a password?**
  If this is the case, then each user must ask for the password from the owner of the network. You still do not know who is connected to the Wi-Fi network, but at least this puts up the first barrier against unwanted guests.

- **Check to see if you have a safe connection.**
  When you send or view sensitive information over the Internet, when you bank online or use webmail for instance, check to see if the connection is safe. You will see 'https://' as prefix in the address bar instead of 'http://'.

- **Make sure your settings for automatic transfer, such as by Bluetooth or synchronization, have been turned off.**
  You can turn off Bluetooth in the *Settings* app. Synchronization settings can be adjusted in the apps that use it, for instance *Email*.

- **Always be aware of the security risks with public Wi-Fi networks.**
  Avoid actions in which personal data or login credentials are being used. If you are transferring sensitive information it is always better to use a secured mobile data connection or a private Wi-Fi connection that you trust.

1.11 Tips

Tip

Sleep mode

The default setting on your tablet will automatically lock it after two minutes of inactivity and put it into sleep mode. This setting will save battery power. But if you prefer to have your tablet remain active a little longer (or shorter) you can adjust the display settings like this:

☞ **Open the *Settings* app** 🦶³

☞ **Tap** 🔆 **Display**

☞ **Tap**
Sleep
After 30 seconds of inactivity

In this window you can set the amount of time of inactivity to elapse before the tablet goes to sleep:

☞ **Tap the desired setting**

ⓥ Tip

Set sounds

Your tablet makes a noise when various events occur, for example, when you receive an email or a message, or when you use the keyboard. You can determine which sounds you do and do not want to hear. You do this in the *Settings* screen:

☞ **Open the *Settings* screen** ⓑ³

👉 **Tap** 🔊 **Sound**

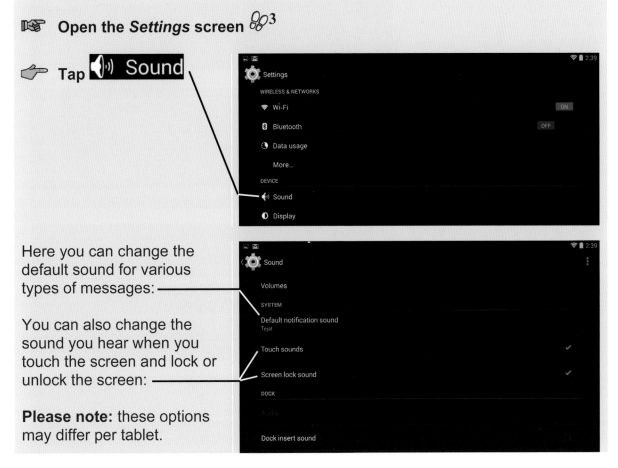

Here you can change the default sound for various types of messages: ⎯

You can also change the sound you hear when you touch the screen and lock or unlock the screen: ⎯

Please note: these options may differ per tablet.

ⓥ Tip

Secure with a pattern

Your tablet is protected automatically from unintentional entries. When you turn on your tablet, you simply drag the padlock across the screen to unlock the device. But anyone else using your tablet can do this as well. You can add an extra layer of security to your tablet, for instance, by requiring a PIN code, a password, or a pattern to unlock it. This is how you secure the tablet with a pattern:

☞ **Open the *Settings* app** ⓑ³

- Continue on the next page -

☞ **Swipe upwards over the screen**

☞ **Tap** 🔒 **Security**

☞ **Tap** **Screen lock** Slide

You will see various types of security measures to choose from:

☞ **Tap** Pattern

☞ **Drag a pattern with which you connect at least four circles**

☞ **Tap** Continue

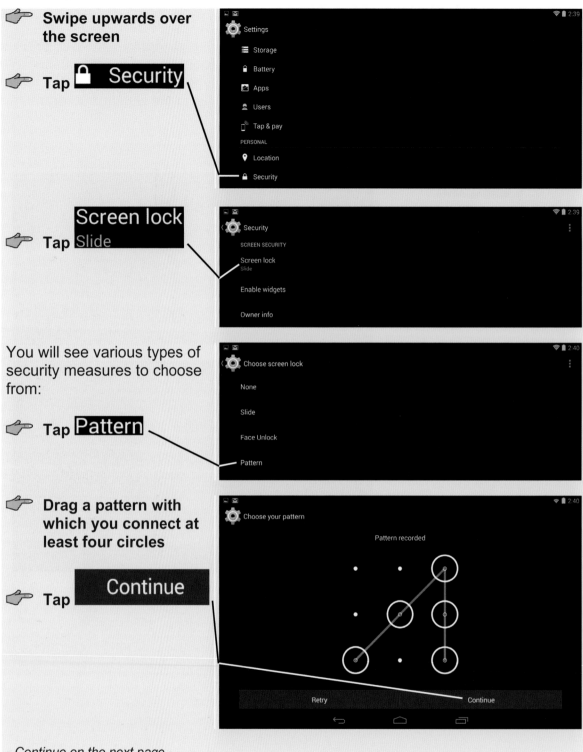

- Continue on the next page -

☞ **Drag the same pattern once more**

☞ **Tap** Confirm

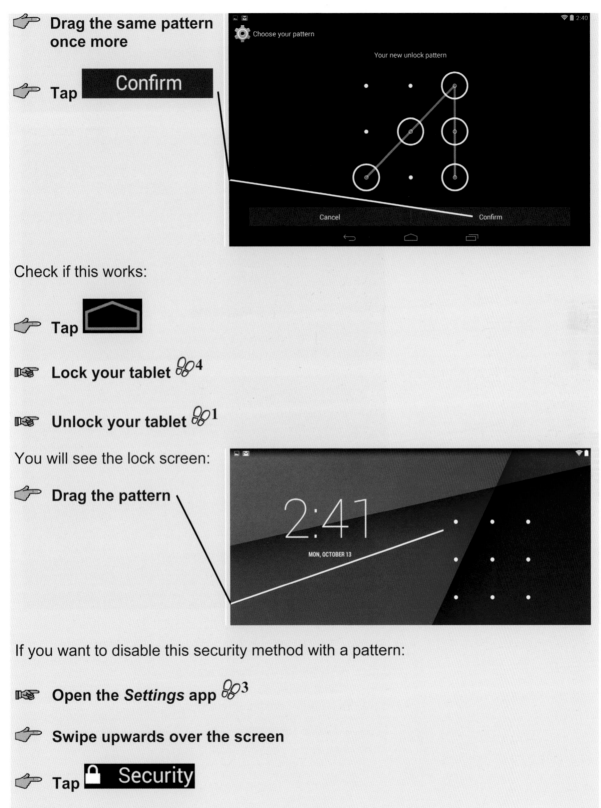

Check if this works:

☞ **Tap** ⌂

☞ **Lock your tablet** 🐾4

☞ **Unlock your tablet** 🐾1

You will see the lock screen:

☞ **Drag the pattern**

If you want to disable this security method with a pattern:

☞ **Open the *Settings* app** 🐾3

☞ **Swipe upwards over the screen**

☞ **Tap** 🔒 Security

- Continue on the next page -

👉 **Tap** Screen lock Pattern

👉 **Drag the pattern**

Now you can select a different safety method, or no method at all:

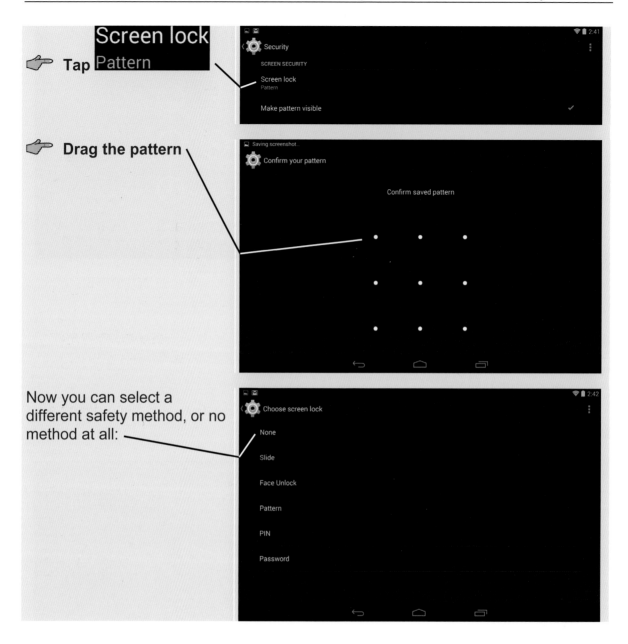

2. Using Email on Your Tablet

An *Android 4.4* tablet will often have two different email apps. These are the *Gmail* and *Email* apps. The *Gmail* app is developed especially for *Google Mail* accounts, also known as *Gmail*. The *Email* app lets you use the services from other email providers.

Both of these apps will allow you to write, send, and receive email in pretty much the same manner as you have become accustomed to on a regular computer.

In this chapter you will learn how to use the *Email* app. You will start by adding an existing email account to your tablet, so that you can start using the app right away.

You will then get acquainted with the keyboard and learn how to type text, numbers, and special characters on the screen of your tablet. You will learn how to select, copy, and paste text and how to use the *Auto correction* function.

In just a short time, you will see how easy it is to create, send, receive, and delete an email on your tablet.

In this chapter you will learn how to:

- set up an email account in the *Email* app;
- write and send an email message;
- receive an email;
- move an email to the *Trash*;
- permanently delete an email.

Please note:

The screens you see on your own tablet may look different from the images in this book. The buttons may also have a different name or look a little different. Always search for a similar button or function. The basic operations will remain the same.

2.1 Adding an Email Account to th

In this section you are going to open the *Email* app
from an Internet service provider such as AOL or \
need to have the server data, user name, and pas:
you by your Internet provider. If you have an email
hotmail.com, outlook.com, live.com, or gmail.com,

☞ Unlock or turn on the tablet 👣¹

The *Email* app may already be placed on the home a
favorites tray. If that is not the case, you can open the
overview:

☞ Tap

If this is the first time you are
opening the apps overview,
you may see this screen first:

☞ If necessary, tap

OK

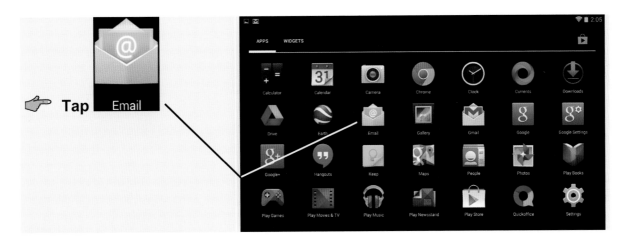

☞ Tap **Email**

➥ Please note:

You need to select an email provider for your tablet. If your email provider is not shown in the list of providers, you will need to select the *POP3/IMAP* option.

You will see a screen where you need to enter some basic information about your email account. You will be using the onscreen keyboard to do this:

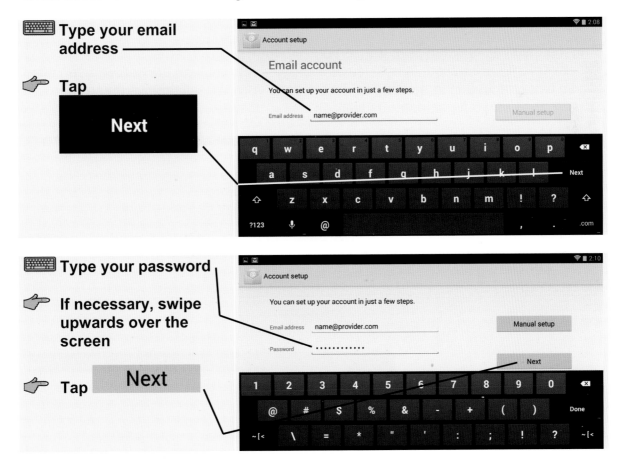

⌨ **Type your email address**

☞ **Tap**

Next

⌨ **Type your password**

☞ **If necessary, swipe upwards over the screen**

☞ **Tap** **Next**

Please note:

If you are using an email address that ends in live.com, outlook.com, hotmail.com, or gmail.com, you can skip the next few steps.
In this case, you will only see a screen with the account options, and a screen where you can change the account name. When you have finished entering the required information, the email account is set up automatically. You can continue on the bottom of page 58.

Now you are going to choose between an *IMAP* and a *POP3* email account:

- IMAP stands for *Internet Message Access Protocol*. This means that you will be managing your email messages on the mail server. Read messages will remain stored on the mail server until you delete them. IMAP is useful if you manage your email on multiple computers or devices. Your mailbox will look the same on each device. If you create any folders to arrange your email messages, the same folders will appear on each computer and on your tablet. If you want to use IMAP, you will need to set up your email account as an IMAP account on all your devices.

- POP stands for *Post Office Protocol*, which is the traditional way of managing email messages. Once you have retrieved your email, the messages will immediately be deleted from the server. Although on your tablet, the default setting for POP3 accounts is to leave a copy of your mail on the server, even after you have retrieved the messages. This means you can still receive these messages on your computer as well.

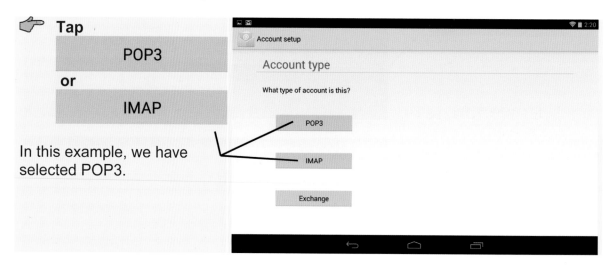

☞ **Tap**

> **POP3**
>
> **or**
>
> **IMAP**

In this example, we have selected POP3.

Enter the data provided to you by your email provider:

By Username, type your user name

If necessary, type your password by Password

Swipe upwards over the screen a bit

By Server, type the name of the incoming mail server

Tap Next

By SMTP server, type the name of the outgoing mail server

Swipe upwards over the screen

Uncheck the box by Require signin

Tap Next

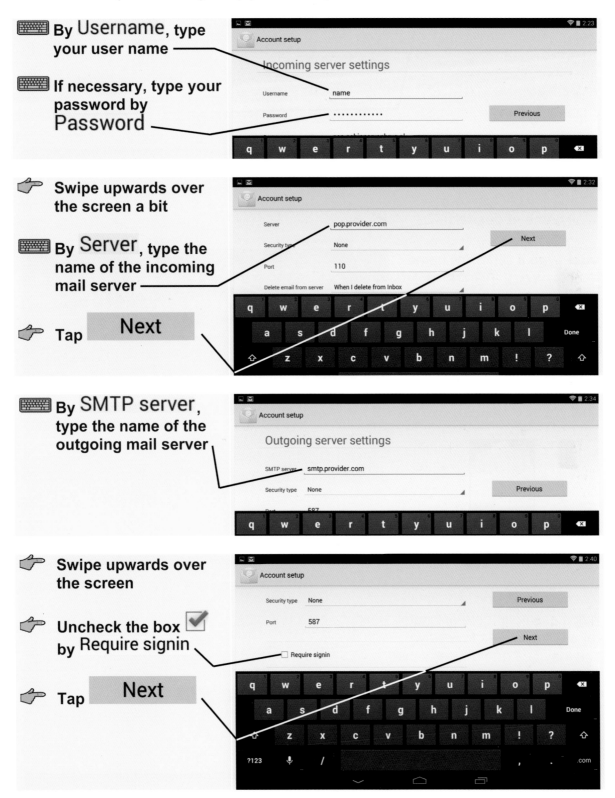

☞ **Tap** Next

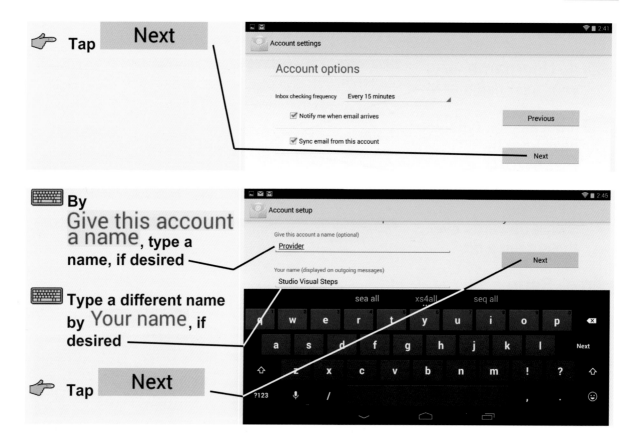

⌨ **By Give this account a name, type a name, if desired**

⌨ **Type a different name by Your name, if desired**

☞ **Tap** Next

Now you see the apps overview:

☞ **Tap** Email

You will see the screen of the *Email* app:

In this example there are not yet any messages to receive. You may see one or two messages in your own account.

Inbox
Provider

No messages.

2.2 Writing and Sending an Email Message

To get used to using email on your tablet you can practice by writing and sending an email to yourself. You can also try out the automatic spell checker:

In the upper-right corner of the screen:

☞ **Tap** 📧➕

A new message is opened.

⌨ **By** To **, type your own email address**

💡 **Tip**

Contacts
If any contacts have been added to the *People* app, you will see a list of names and corresponding email addresses, as soon as you have typed the first two letters of a name.
You can quickly add one of these email addresses by tapping the desired name. In *Chapter 4 The Standard Apps on Your Tablet* you will learn how to add more contacts to the *People* app.

☞ **Tap** Subject

Type: Test

While you are typing, the bar above the keyboard will display suggestions for the word you are typing:

This function is called *Correction suggestions* and is part of the *Auto correction* function. While you are typing, certain words are suggested on the basis of the letters you are currently typing. This may save you a lot of time with your typing. You can accept the suggestion in the middle (with the dotted line) by tapping the space bar. You can accept the other suggestions by tapping them. Just try this with the first part of the word 'computer'.

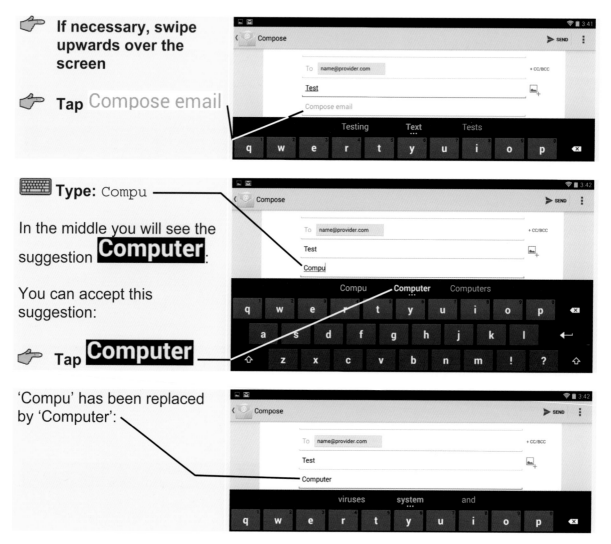

☞ **If necessary, swipe upwards over the screen**

☞ **Tap** Compose email

Type: Compu

In the middle you will see the suggestion **Computer**.

You can accept this suggestion:

☞ **Tap** **Computer**

'Compu' has been replaced by 'Computer':

The nice thing about this function is that it can automatically correct many spelling errors. Just see what happens when you intentionally type a spelling error:

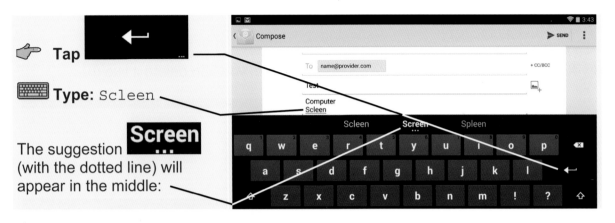

Tap

Type: Scleen

The suggestion **Screen** (with the dotted line) will appear in the middle:

You can accept the suggestion in the middle (with the dotted line) by tapping the

space bar or after the word. Your entry will then be corrected. You may not even notice your mistake.

Tap the space bar

Now the word 'Screen' has been inserted into the email:

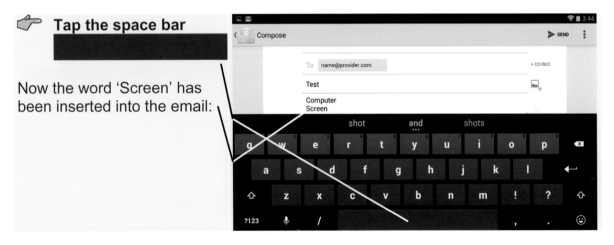

Tip
Accept a correction
A suggested correction will also be accepted if you type a period, comma, or other punctuation mark.

Tip
Select your own entry or another suggestion
If the word that is suggested is not correct, you can select your own entry in the email message by tapping it. You can do the same for the suggestions that are not shown in the middle.

Tip

Disable correction suggestions
In the *Tips* at the end of this chapter you can read how to disable the *Correction suggestions* function while you are typing.

If you are not satisfied with the text you have typed, you can delete it like this:

Place and hold your finger on 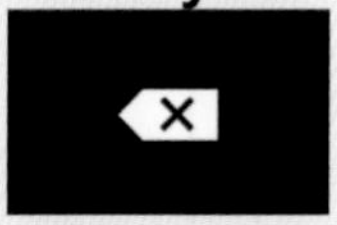 **until both lines have been deleted**

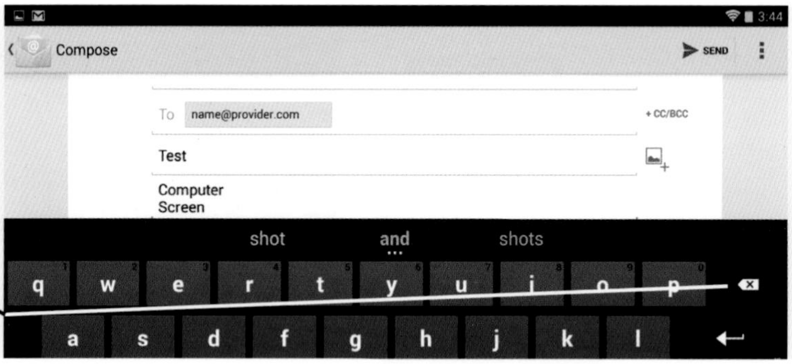

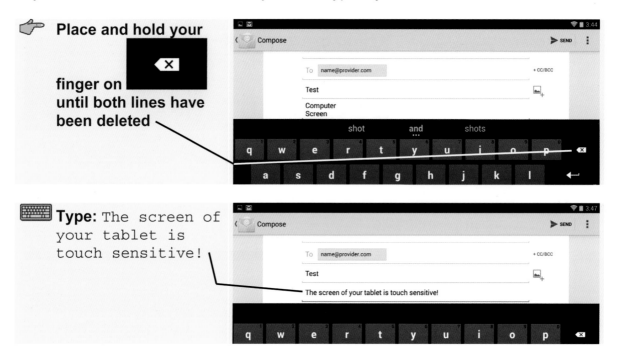

Type: `The screen of your tablet is touch sensitive!`

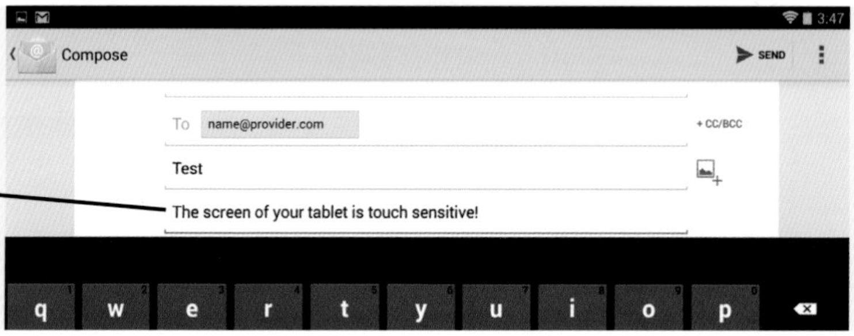

Tip

Unknown word
If the word you type is unknown and no suggestions have been found, the word will sometimes be underlined in red. Then you can do the following:

Tap the word

You will see a number of suggestions for the word:

You can also choose to add the word to the dictionary, or delete it:

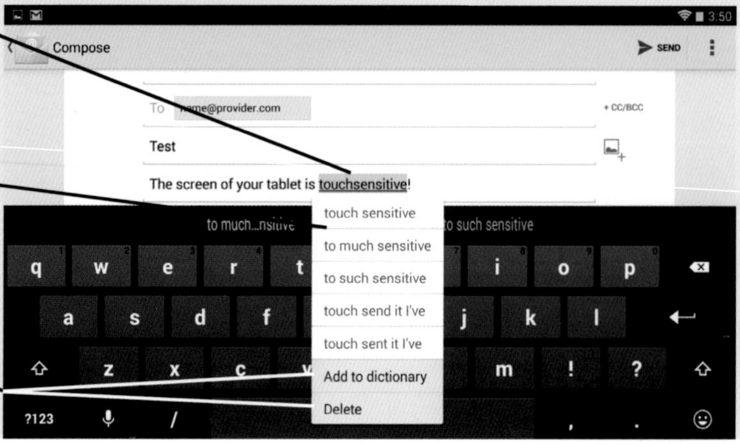

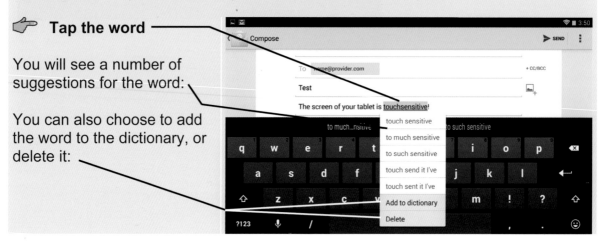

In the *Email* app you can also copy, cut, and paste text. This can be done with a single word, multiple words, or even with the entire text at once. In this example we will use a single word. This is how you select a word:

☞ **Place your finger on the word** The ──

The word will be selected and you will see handles on both sides of the word:

☞ **Release the screen**

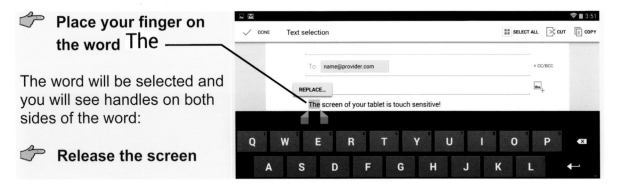

You can adjust the selection by using the handles. Practice selecting the words 'The screen of your tablet':

☞ **Drag the right handle**

across screen of your tablet

Now the text has been selected:

You can cut, copy, or replace the selected words. Practice copying the words:

☞ **Tap** 📋 **COPY**

If you want to cut the text, you tap ✂ **CUT** .

The words have been copied to the clipboard. This is how you paste the words into the text:

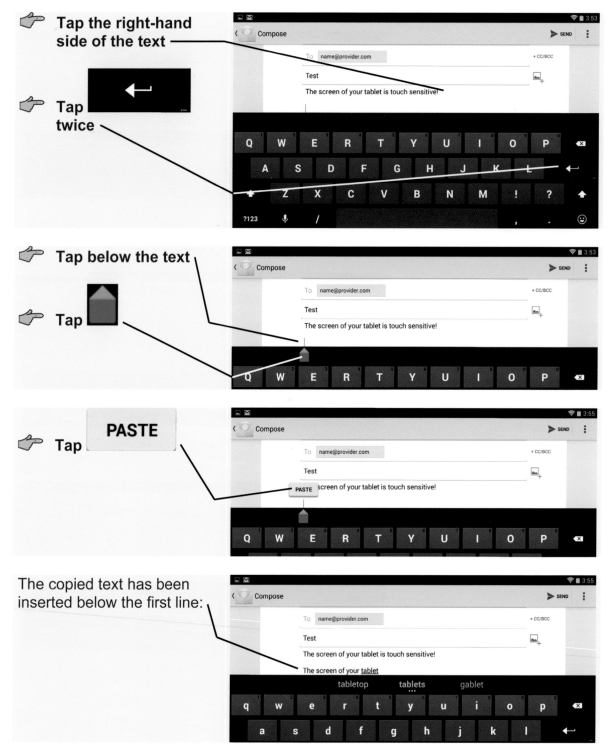

Now you can send your email:

☞ **Tap** ▶ **SEND**

Your email message will be sent.

2.3 Receiving an Email Message

Once you have sent it, your email will be received very soon. It will appear at the top of your *Inbox*:

☞ **Tap the incoming message**

☞ **HELP! I have not received any email.**
If you do not receive an email at once, you can do this:

☞ **Tap** ▪▪▪

☞ **Tap** Refresh

You will see the content of the message:

Tip

Open an attachment

You may sometimes receive an email with an attachment, such as a photo. In the *Tips* at the end of this chapter you can read how to open an attachment.

In the toolbar above the message you will find a number of buttons. This is what they do:

 Mark a message with a star.

 Reply to a message.

 Reply to all the senders.

 Forward a message.

In the upper-right corner of the screen you will find even more buttons. This is what they are for:

 Open a new email message.

 Search the messages.

 Move a message to the *Trash*.

 Mark a message as unread.

 Open the menu.

2.4 Deleting an Email Message

This is how you delete your email:

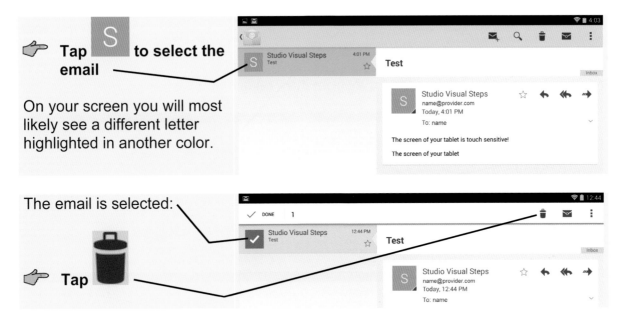

☞ **Tap** to select the email

On your screen you will most likely see a different letter highlighted in another color.

The email is selected:

☞ **Tap**

The email has been moved to the *Trash*. You can verify this:

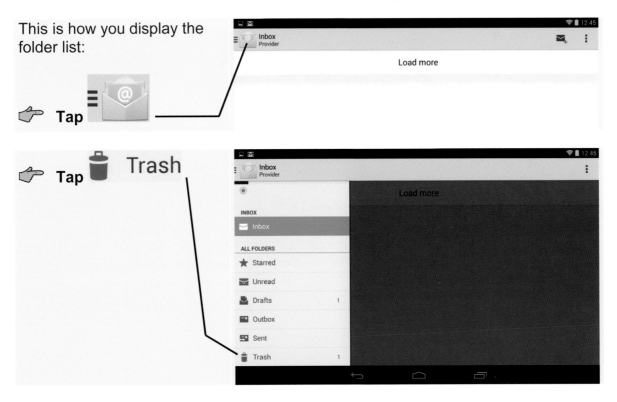

This is how you display the folder list:

☞ **Tap**

☞ **Tap** 🗑 Trash

The deleted message can be found in the *Trash*:

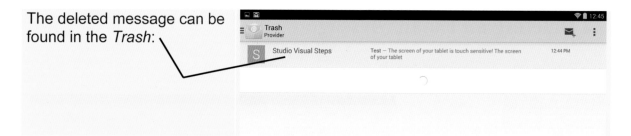

You can permanently delete the email from the *Trash*, if you wish:

☞ **Tap** S **to select the message**

☞ **Tap** 🗑

Now the message has been permanently deleted.

☞ **Go to the home screen** 👣²

☞ **If desired, lock or turn off the tablet** 👣⁴

In this chapter you have become acquainted with the *Email* app on your tablet. You have learned how to write, send, receive, and delete an email message.

2.5 Background Information

Dictionary

Account	A combination of a user name and a password, that provides access to a specific service.
Correction suggestions	A function that displays suggestions for the word you are currently typing.
Email	One of the standard apps on the tablet for sending and receiving email. You can add accounts from different service providers to this app.
Fetch	The traditional way of retrieving new email messages. You open your email program and the server is contacted. You can set up your email program to check for new messages at regular intervals, when it is opened.
Gmail	A free email service offered by *Google,* the manufacturer of the well-known search engine. The app in which you send or receive email with *Gmail* has the same name.
Inbox	A folder in which you can view the email messages you have received.
People	One of the standard apps on your tablet for viewing, adding and maintaining a list of contacts.
Push	When push has been enabled and is supported by your Internet service provider, all new email messages will immediately be sent to your email app by the mail server, once they have arrived, even if your email app has not been opened and your tablet is locked.
Signature	A standard salutation that is inserted below your outgoing email messages.
Trash	A folder in which your deleted messages are stored. A message is permanently deleted only when you delete it from the *Trash.*

Source: User manual Polaroid tablet and Gmail

2.6 Tips

 Tip

Push or fetch

If you use an email program on your computer, you will be accustomed to retrieving your email through the *fetch* function. You open your email program and establish a connection with the mail server in order to retrieve new messages. You can set up the mail program to check for new emails at regular intervals, provided the program has been opened.

The *Email* app works with the *push* function. New email messages will be sent to the app, immediately after they have been received by the mail server, even if the *Email* app has not been opened and your tablet is locked. If your tablet has been turned off completely, you will not receive any email.

☞ **Open the *Settings* app** ⌘³

This is how you view the synchronization settings for the *Email* app:

Please note: depending on your type of tablet, you may not be able to turn off the automatic synchronization function.

👉 **Swipe upwards over the screen**

👉 **By ACCOUNTS, tap the type of email account you are using** ———

👉 **Tap your email account**

👉 **Uncheck the box** ✔️ **by**
Email
Last synced 10/16/2014

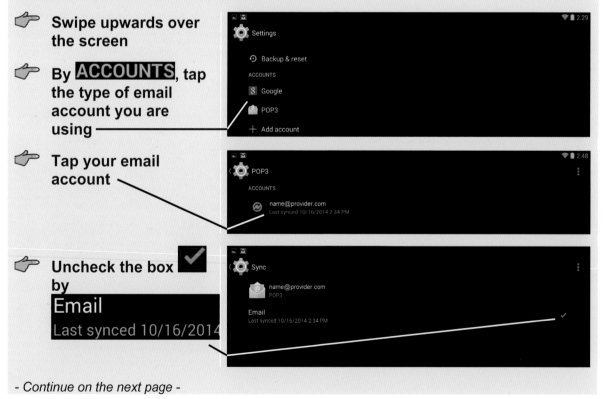

- Continue on the next page -

Now your email will no longer be synchronized automatically. You can also fetch your email manually right from the *Email* app. When the *Email* app is open:

☞ **Tap** ⋮

☞ **Tap** Refresh

💡 **Tip**

Add a signature to the messages you send
You can insert a standard text below each email message you send. For instance, a standard salutation or your name and address. This text is called your *signature*. Here is how you add a signature:

☞ **Tap** ⋮

☞ **Tap** Settings

☞ **Tap your email address**

Signature
☞ **Tap** Not set

⌨ **Type your signature**

☞ **Tap**

OK

Inbox
Provider

Refresh
Settings
Send feedback

Settings   ADD ACCOUNT

General settings

Provider
name@provider.com

name@provider.com

Account name
Provider

Your name
Studio Visual Steps

Signature
Not set

Signature

With kind regards,

Cancel   OK

- Continue on the next page -

To go back to the *Inbox*:

☞ **If necessary, tap**

☞ **Tap**

💡 **Tip**

Disable correction suggestions

The *Correction suggestions* function on your tablet can sometimes lead to unwanted corrections. The dictionary may not recognize all the words you type, but will still try to suggest a word. This can result in some weird or even embarrassing corrections, especially if you have made a typing error without noticing it. Without really intending to accept the correction you may have typed a period, comma, or blank space, and because of this the suggestion was accepted. If you would like to prevent this from happening, you can disable the *Correction suggestions* function:

☞ **Open the *Settings* app** 🦶³

☞ **If necessary, wipe upwards over the screen**

☞ **If necessary, tap**
[A.] Language & input

☞ **By Google Keyboard English (US),**

tap ⇄

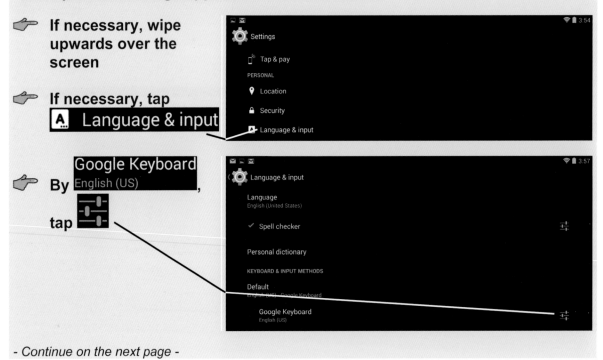

- Continue on the next page -

You will see various keyboard settings:

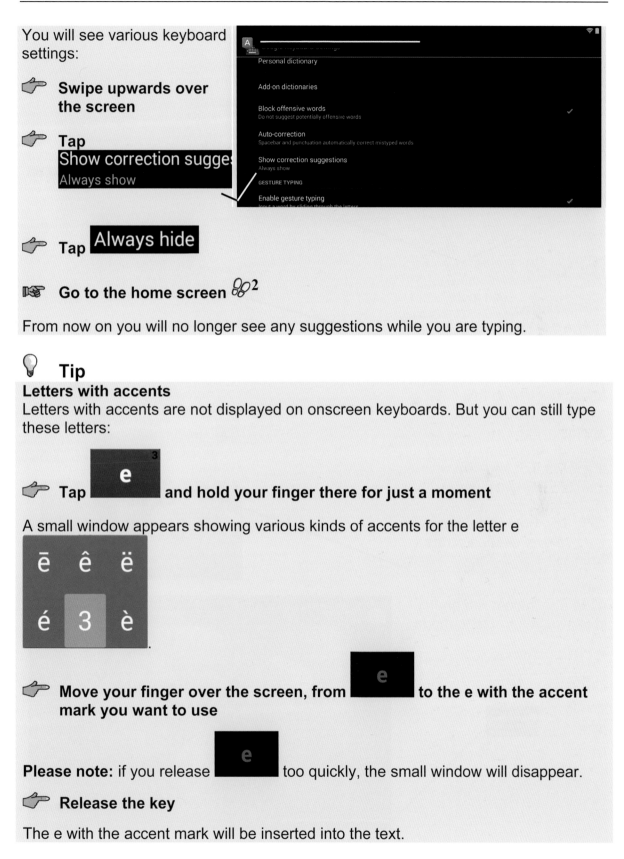

☞ **Swipe upwards over the screen**

☞ **Tap**
Show correction sugge
Always show

☞ **Tap** **Always hide**

☞ **Go to the home screen** ⅋²

From now on you will no longer see any suggestions while you are typing.

💡 **Tip**
Letters with accents
Letters with accents are not displayed on onscreen keyboards. But you can still type these letters:

☞ **Tap** e³ **and hold your finger there for just a moment**

A small window appears showing various kinds of accents for the letter e

ē ê ë
é 3 è

☞ **Move your finger over the screen, from** e **to the e with the accent mark you want to use**

Please note: if you release e **too quickly, the small window will disappear.**

☞ **Release the key**

The e with the accent mark will be inserted into the text.

Tip
Open an attachment
You may sometimes receive an email with an attachment, such as a photo. To open the attachment, you first need to open the email message:

☞ **Open the email message** 🔖16

You can recognize an attachment by the paperclip

icon   :

☞ **Tap**

　　📎　Load more

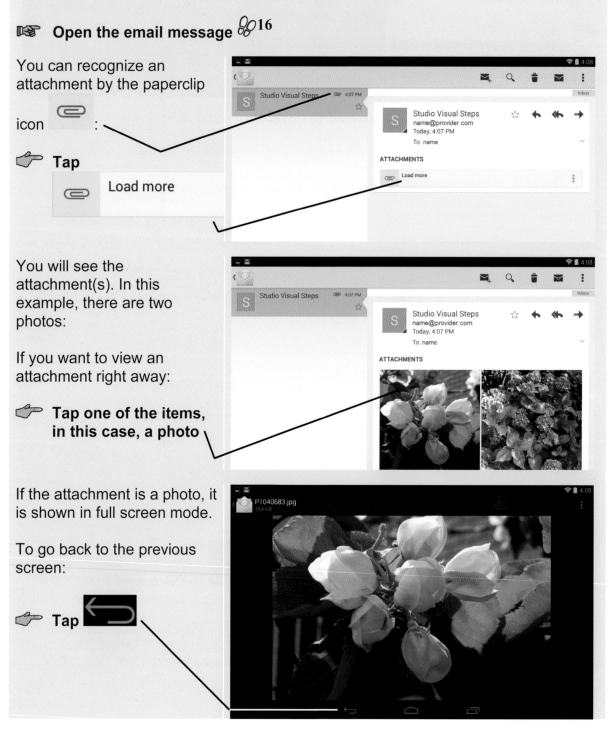

You will see the attachment(s). In this example, there are two photos:

If you want to view an attachment right away:

☞ **Tap one of the items, in this case, a photo**

If the attachment is a photo, it is shown in full screen mode.

To go back to the previous screen:

☞ **Tap** 🔙

3. Surfing with Your Tablet

Your *Android* tablet may contain more than one app to browse the web. In this chapter you will get acquainted with the default web browsing app called *Chrome*. This app lets you browse and search the Internet on your tablet with ease. If you are accustomed to using Internet on a regular computer, you will soon see that surfing on your tablet is just as easy. The main difference is there is no need to use a mouse. You use touch gestures instead to navigate through a website.

First, you will learn how to open a web page, and how to zoom in and out. Then you learn the various methods for scrolling. You will also learn how to open links (also called hyperlinks), switch between open web pages, save bookmarks, and search the Internet.

If you are busy surfing the Internet, and want to stop for a moment to quickly answer an email in the *Email* app or adjust a setting in the *Settings* app, you do not need to worry. When you are finished you can return to the web page right where you left off. Switching between apps is effortless, because your *Android* tablet has multitasking capabilities. In this chapter you will soon discover how easy it is to switch between web pages and your recently opened apps.

In this chapter you will learn how to:

- open the *Chrome* app;
- open a web page;
- zoom in and zoom out;
- scroll;
- open a link on a web page;
- open a link on a new tab;
- add a bookmark;
- search;
- switch between recently used apps.

Please note:

The screens you see on your own tablet may look different from the images in this book. The buttons may also have a different name or look a little different. Always search for a similar button or function. The basic operations will remain the same.

3.1 Opening the Chrome App

This is how you open *Chrome*, the app for browsing and searching the Internet:

☞ **Unlock or turn on the tablet** ✂¹

You can open the *Chrome* app from the home screen:

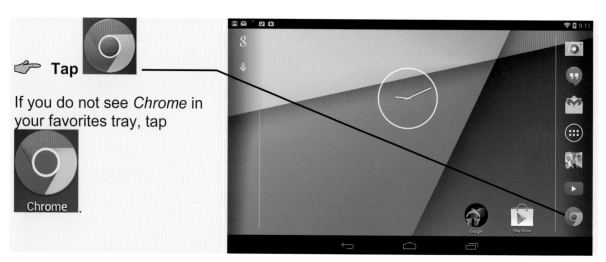

☞ **Tap**

If you do not see *Chrome* in your favorites tray, tap

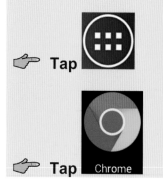

Chrome .

🩹 **HELP! The Chrome app is not visible on the home screen.**

If the *Chrome* app is not shown on the home screen:

☞ **Tap**

☞ **Tap** Chrome

If necessary, tap
ACCEPT & CONTINUE

You can allow *Google Chrome* to be associated with your *Google* account and take advantage of *Google's* sharing and syncing options. But for now, this is not needed:

If necessary, tap
NO THANKS

You will see the *Chrome* home page:

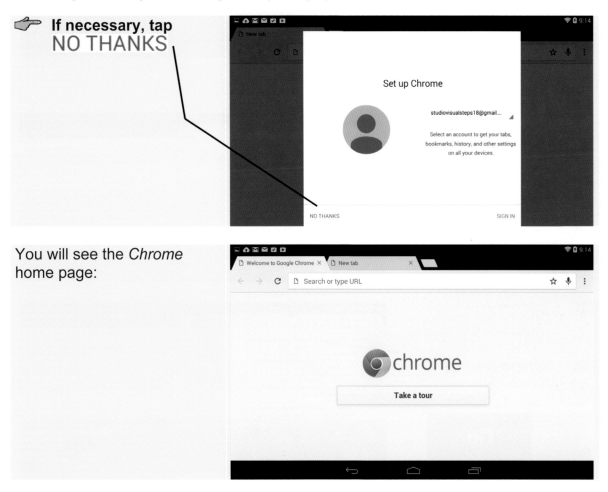

3.2 Opening a Web Page

In order to type a web address, you need to display the onscreen keyboard:

☞ **Tap the address bar**

You will see the onscreen keyboard:

For practicing purposes, you can open the Visual Steps website:

Type: www.

You will see several suggestions:

The more letters of the web address you type, the more specific the suggestions will become.

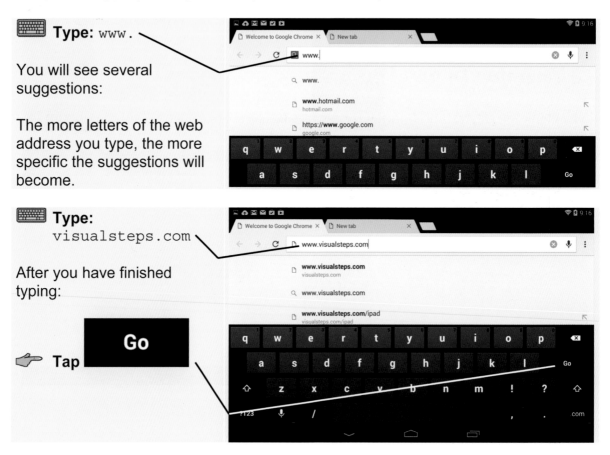

Type: visualsteps.com

After you have finished typing:

☞ **Tap** Go

💡 **Tip**

Use a suggestion

You can simply tap [www.visualsteps.com / visualsteps.com] in the suggestions list, if it already appears in the list.

You will see the Visual Steps website:

3.3 Zooming In and Out

If you think the letters and images on a website are a bit too small, you can zoom in. You can do this using your thumb and index fingers. Set them on the spot that you want to enlarge:

👉 **Slowly spread you thumb and index finger away from each other on the screen**

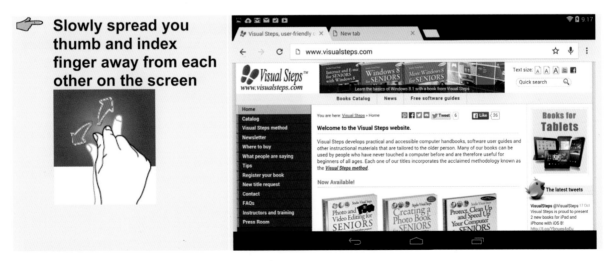

You will see that you are zooming in on the page:

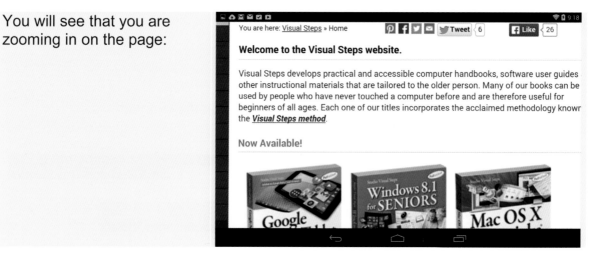

You can zoom out again by making the same gesture in reverse:

☞ **Move your thumb and index finger towards each other on the**

screen

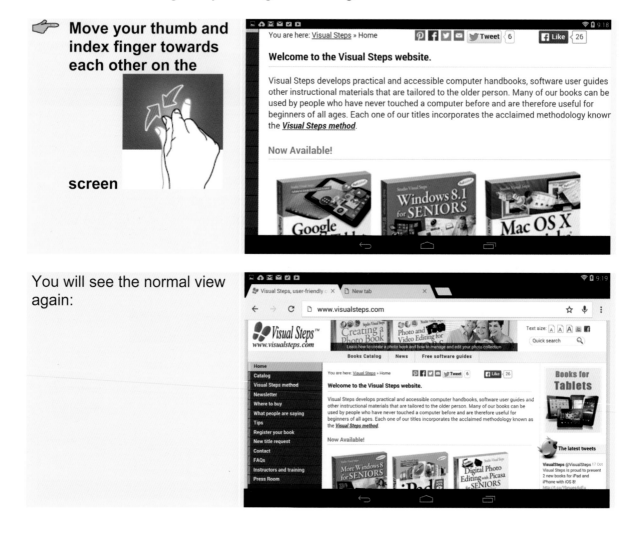

You will see the normal view again:

Tip

Zooming by double-tapping

Depending on the type of tablet you have, you may also be able to zoom in and out by double-tapping the screen. To zoom in:

☞ **Double-tap the screen**

You will see that the web page is displayed much larger. To zoom out again:

☞ **Double-tap the screen**

3.4 Scrolling

Scrolling means navigating through a web page. You use scrolling to view the content of a longer web page that is off screen. On your tablet you use your fingers to scroll through a web page:

☞ **Drag your finger upwards over the**

screen

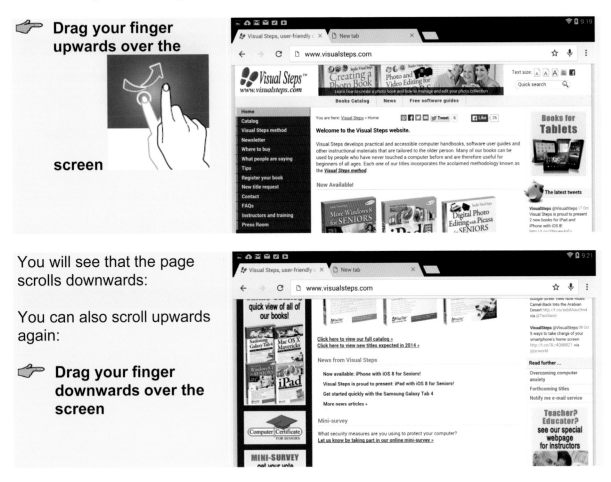

You will see that the page scrolls downwards:

You can also scroll upwards again:

☞ **Drag your finger downwards over the screen**

💡 Tip

Scrolling sideways
On a wide web page, you can scroll sideways by pressing and holding the screen with your finger, and dragging it from right to left or from left to right.

If you quickly want to scroll through a long page, you can use a swiping gesture:

👉 **Move your finger upwards, in a swiping gesture, over the screen**

This gesture is also called flicking.

You will see the bottom part of the web page:

💡 Tip

Move in other directions
You can just as easily scroll upwards, or to the left or right, by swiping in another direction.

This is how you quickly return to the top of the page:

Swipe downwards over the screen

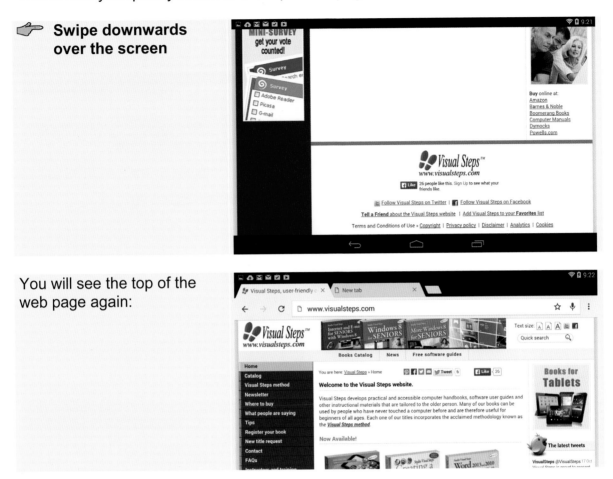

You will see the top of the web page again:

3.5 Opening a Link on a Web Page

If a web page contains a link, you can open the link by tapping it. Just try it:

Tap **Where to buy**

HELP! I cannot tap the link.

If you find it difficult to tap the right link, you can zoom in first. The links will then be displayed a little larger, making it easier to tap them.

The web page with information about where to find the books from Visual Steps will be opened:

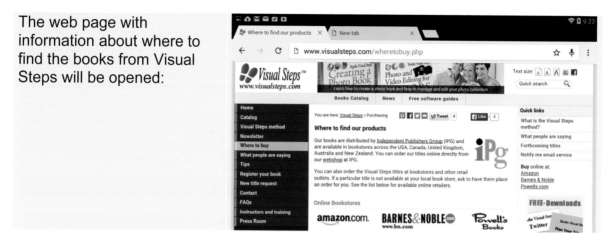

3.6 Opening a Link on a New Tab

You can also open a link on a new tab:

☞ **Place your finger on**
Forthcoming titles

You will see a menu:

☞ **Tap**
Open in new tab

http://www.visualsteps.com/new-titles.php

Open in new tab

Open in incognito tab

Copy link address

The web page for this link has been opened in a new tab. To view the tab:

Tap Expected new titles,

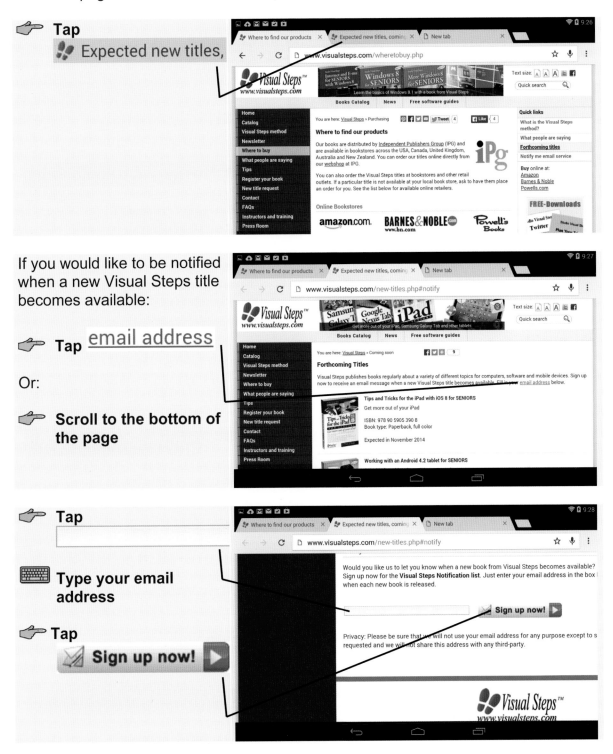

If you would like to be notified when a new Visual Steps title becomes available:

Tap email address

Or:

Scroll to the bottom of the page

Tap

Type your email address

Tap Sign up now!

You will receive an email when a new book is published. This is a notification service from Visual Steps and there are no strings attached.

This is how you close an
open tab:

☞ **Tap** ✕

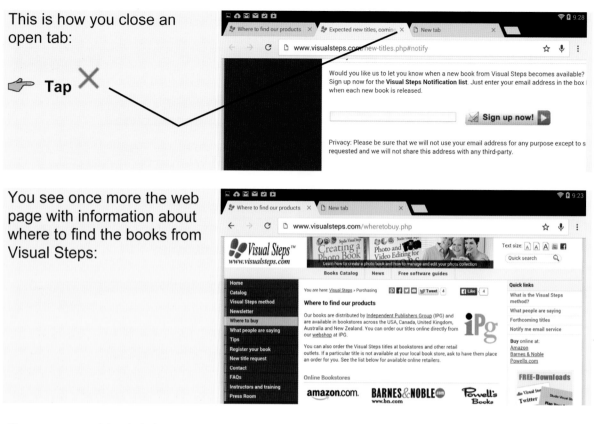

You see once more the web
page with information about
where to find the books from
Visual Steps:

Open a new, blank tab:

☞ **Tap** 🗋 New tab

🩹 **HELP! I do not see** 🗋 New tab .

You can also open a new tab like this:

☞ **Tap** ▱

You will see the new tab:

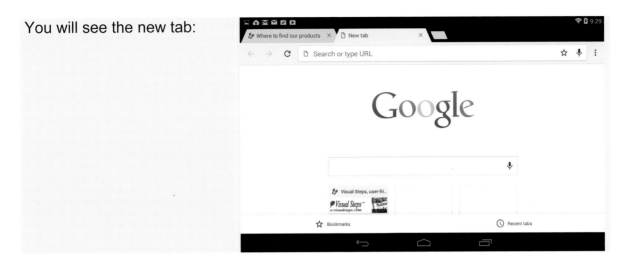

3.7 Adding a Bookmark

If you want to visit a web page more often, you can add a *bookmark*. A bookmark refers to a website that you have saved, so that you can view it whenever you want. One of the bonuses of creating a bookmark is that you do not need to type the entire website address each time you want to visit it. This is how you add a bookmark:

☞ **Go to the first tab** ℰ𝒪⁵

👉 Tap **Home**

In the address bar:

👉 Tap ☆

In the *Add bookmark* window you can enter another, easily identifiable name for this web page, if you wish. For now this is not necessary.
To save the bookmark:

☞ Tap **Save**

Add bookmark

Name
s, user-friendly computer and software books for older individuals

URL
http://www.visualsteps.com/index.php

Folder
Mobile bookmarks

Cancel   Save

The web page has been added to your bookmarks. You can verify this:

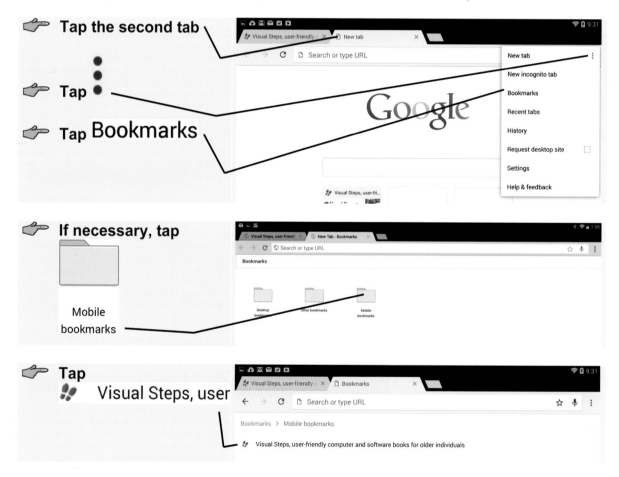

☞ Tap the second tab

☞ Tap

☞ Tap **Bookmarks**

☞ If necessary, tap

Mobile bookmarks

☞ Tap
Visual Steps, user

You will see the Visual Steps website again.

3.8 Searching

In *Chrome* you can also use the address bar as a search box. You can enter a keyword or phrase directly in the address bar:

☞ **Tap the address bar**

⌨ **Type:** android

While you are typing, you will see an assortment of suggestions for the keywords. You can go to one of these suggestions by tapping it. For now this is not necessary.

To use your own keyword:

☞ **Tap** **Go**

You will see the search results:

If you want to view a result, just tap the link. For now this is not necessary.

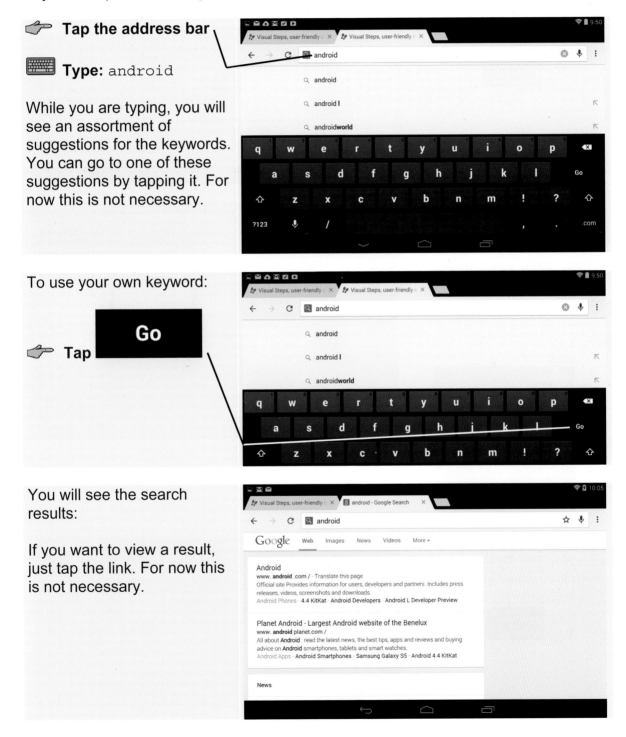

3.9 Switching Between Recently Used Apps

You can use a button at the bottom of your screen to switch between recently used apps. Just give it a try:

At the bottom of the screen:

👉 **Tap**

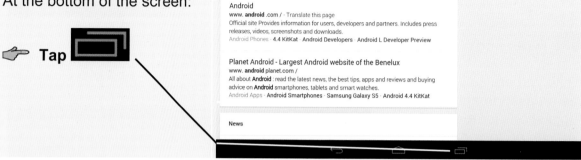

You will see a menu with recently used apps:

Please note: you may see other recently used apps on your own screen.

👉 **Tap an app, for example**

You will see the *Settings* app:

To go to another app:

👉 **Tap**

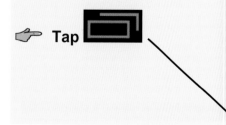

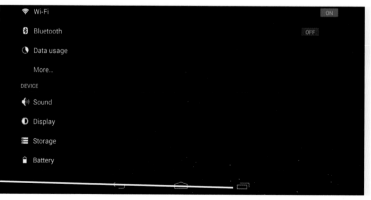

Tap

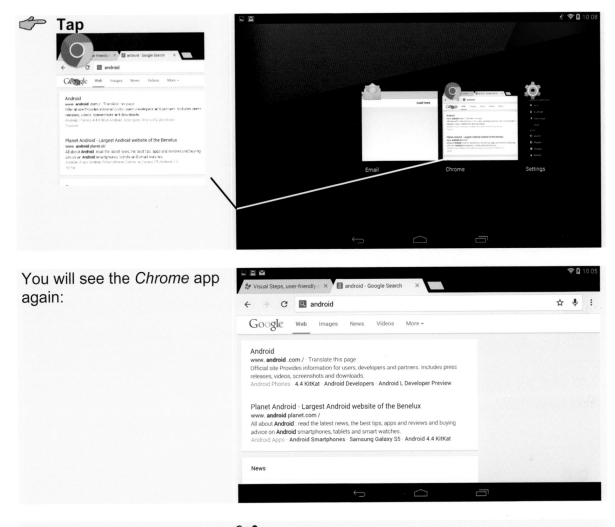

You will see the *Chrome* app again:

☞ **Go to the home screen** $\mathscr{O}\mathscr{O}^2$

☞ **If desired, lock or turn off the tablet** $\mathscr{O}\mathscr{O}^4$

3.10 Background Information

Dictionary

Bookmark	A reference to a web address that has been stored in a list, so that you can view the web page later on.
Chrome	A web browsing app on your tablet to browse and search the Internet.
Cookies	Data that the server sends to the browser, in order to save it and send it back to the server when the user visits the website again. Many European countries require websites to inform their visitors of the use of cookies and of the way they are being used.
Google	*Google,* known mainly as a search engine, also offers many other types of online services, such as *Google Maps, Chrome,* and *Gmail* (an email application).
Link, hyperlink	A link is a navigational tool on a web page, intended to lead the user to the information when the link is clicked or tapped. A link may be a bit of text, a photo or other graphical image, a button, or an icon. Links are also called hyperlinks.
Scroll	Moving a web page upwards or downwards across the screen, or to the left or right. You do this on a tablet by using various touching maneuvers with your fingers.
Zoom in	Take a closer look at an item. The letters and images become larger.
Zoom out	View an item from a distance. The letters and images become smaller.

Source: User manual Polaroid tablet, Wikipedia

3.11 Tips

💡 Tip

Delete browsing history

The browsing history contains data and information about the websites you have recently visited. You can delete this information, by deleting the browsing history:

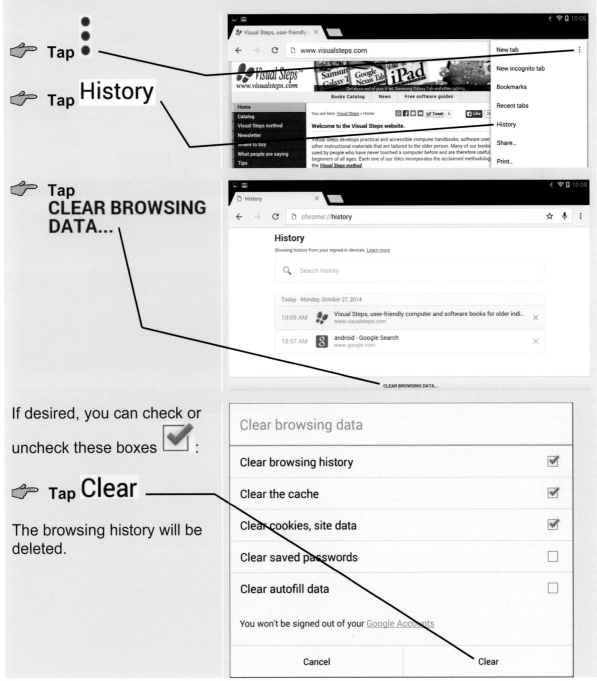

👉 Tap ⋮

👉 Tap History

👉 Tap
CLEAR BROWSING
DATA...

If desired, you can check or uncheck these boxes ☑️:

👉 Tap Clear

The browsing history will be deleted.

🔅 Tip

Voice search

Your tablet is equipped with the *Voice search* function. You can use a verbal search command, for instance, to search for relevant web pages.

In the address bar:

👉 Tap 🎤

👉 Speak loudly and clearly when you enter your search command

You will see the search results:

👉 If desired, tap a link

💡 **Tip**

Google Search
On the home screen, you can open the *Google Search* app

by tapping :

Most likely, you will eventually end up in the *Chrome* app. The first time you open *Google Search*, you will see a number of screens regarding *Google Now*. You can find more information about *Google Now* in the *Tips* at the end of *Chapter 4 The Standard Apps on Your Tablet*.

💡 **Tip**

Delete a bookmark
If you no longer want to use a particular bookmark, you can delete it like this:

☞ **Place your finger on the bookmark you want to delete**

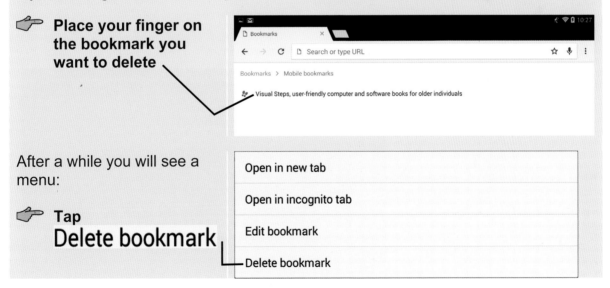

After a while you will see a menu:

☞ **Tap**
Delete bookmark

Open in new tab

Open in incognito tab

Edit bookmark

Delete bookmark

Tip

Signing in to Chrome

In the first part of this chapter you were asked if you wanted to associate *Chrome* with your *Google* account. You skipped that step for the time being. By signing in to your *Google* account when you use *Chrome*, your tabs, bookmarks, and more will be saved across all of your devices that use the *Chrome* web browser. If you would like to sign in to *Chrome*, you can do that as follows:

Tap

Tap Settings

Tap
Sign in to Chrome
Sign in to get your tabs, book

Tap Sign in

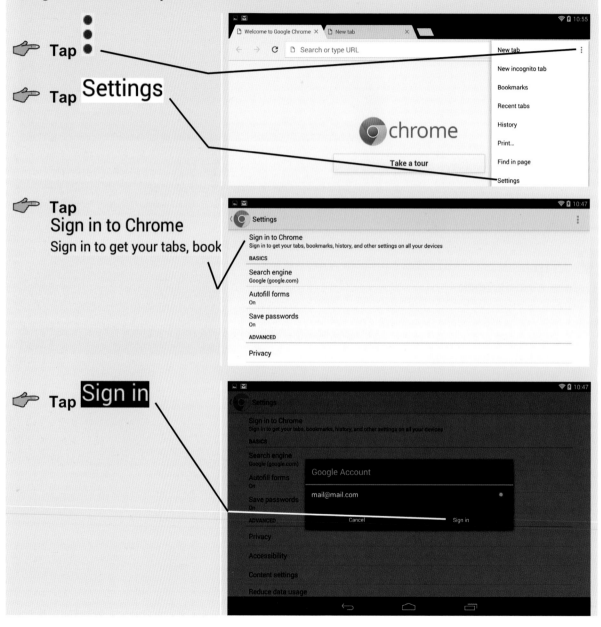

4. The Standard Apps on Your Tablet

Your tablet has plenty of other useful apps besides *Email* and *Chrome*. The *People* app is the standard app for managing information about your contacts. The *Calendar* app can be used to manage appointments and other activities.

The *Maps* app can be used to look up an address or find a well-known location. You can view the location on a regular map or with satellite imagery. Many locations include the *Google Street View* function. This function makes it appear as if you are standing there on the spot. Once a desired location has been found, you can get directions on how to arrive there by car, walking, cycling, or by public transportation.

Google Search is the default app for searching on your tablet. You can use it to search your apps, contacts, messages, and music stored on your tablet, and if you are connected to the Internet, you can search the Internet as well.

In this chapter you will learn how to:

- add, edit, and delete contacts in the *People* app;
- add, edit, and delete appointments in the *Calendar* app;
- determine your current location in the *Maps* app;
- search for a location and get directions;
- search with the *Google Search* app;
- close apps.

Please note:

The screens on your own tablet may look different from the images in this book. The buttons may also have a different name and/or look a little different. Always look for a similar button or function. The basic operations will always remain the same.

4.1 Adding a Contact

Open the *People* app from the apps overview, the screen that displays all the apps installed on your device:

☞ Unlock or turn on the tablet ✂¹

☞ Tap

You will see the *Apps* screen. Not all of the apps may fit onto a single screen. In that case you may need to go to the next screen to find the *People* app:

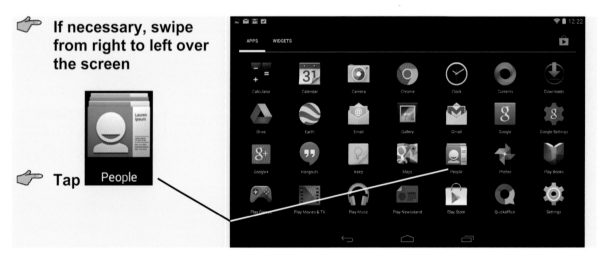

☞ If necessary, swipe from right to left over the screen

☞ Tap People

You can add a new contact like this:

☞ Tap

You may see the window below:

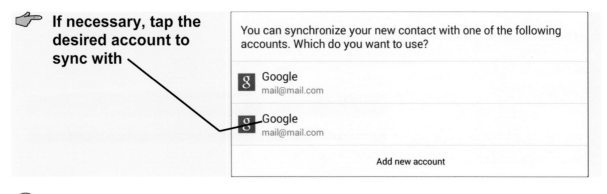

If necessary, tap the desired account to sync with

You can synchronize your new contact with one of the following accounts. Which do you want to use?

Google
mail@mail.com

Google
mail@mail.com

Add new account

💡 **Tip**

Contacts from your Google account
If you have previously added contacts to your *Google* account on another device, such as a mobile phone, they will automatically be synchronized and displayed on your tablet as well, if an Internet connection is available.

You may see the following window:

☞ **If necessary, tap OK**

Your new contact will be synchronized with mail@mail.com.

Add new account   OK

You will see the window where you can add a new contact:

☞ **Tap Name**

In this example, we will be adding a fictitious contact. Of course, you can enter the data for your own contact right away, by using the onscreen keyboard:

⌨ **Type the first and last name of your contact**

☞ **If necessary, swipe upwards over the screen**

☞ **Tap** Phone

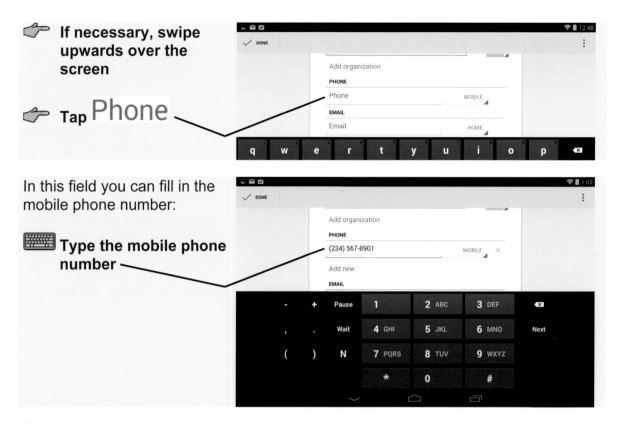

In this field you can fill in the mobile phone number:

⌨ **Type the mobile phone number**

🡖 **Please note:**

When you enter a phone number, the parentheses, spaces and hyphens are inserted automatically.

Add an extra line for another phone number:

☞ **Tap** Add new

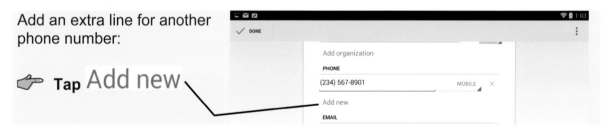

By default, you will see the WORK ◣ label on the line for the extra phone number. You can select another label for the number if you want, for example, a home phone number:

☞ **Tap** WORK ◣

You will see a list of the labels you can choose from:

☞ **Tap** HOME

☞ **Type the home phone number**

You can now add an email address and if desired, the home address as well:

☞ **If necessary, swipe upwards over the screen**

☞ **Tap** Email

☞ **Type your contact's email address**

☞ **Tap** Address

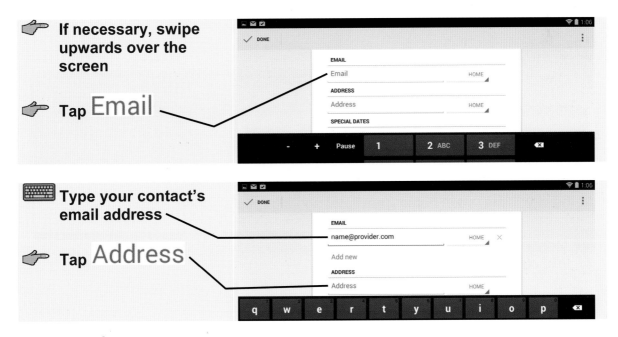

Tip

Select a different label
You can adjust the label by the email address too, for example, from a home email address to a work email address.

Type the number and street name —

To go to the next line:

☞ **Tap**

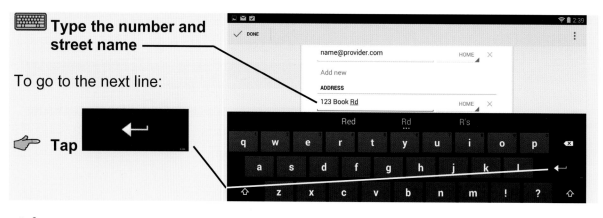

HELP! The street name changes.

If a correction has been found, as you begin to type the street name, the name that you typed will be shown in the middle (with a dotted line), after tapping the space bar, along with other suggestions found. You can prevent this from happening:

☞ **If necessary, tap the correct suggestion**

If desired, you can disable the *Correction suggestions* function. You can read more about this subject in the *Tip Disable correction suggestions* at the end of *Chapter 2 Mailing with Your Tablet*.

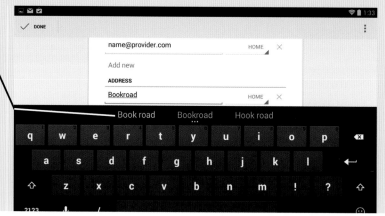

Add the city name, state name (province) and zip (postal) code:

Type the city, state and zip code —

Save the contact:

☞ **Tap** ✓ **DONE** —

Your contact has been added to the list:

☞ **Add two more contacts** 🐾⁶

4.2 Editing a Contact

Once the information for your contacts has been added, you may need to change it every now and then. For example, someone may have a new address, phone number or email address. To open a contact's data from the list of All contacts:

☞ **Tap the desired contact**

☞ **Tap** ✏️

This is how you edit the phone number, for example:

☞ **Swipe upwards over the screen**

☞ **Place your finger on the phone number**

The phone number is selected:

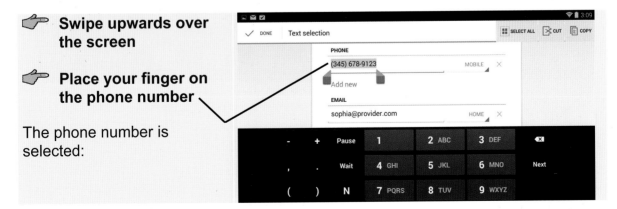

Now you can enter the new phone number:

⌨ Type the new phone number

☞ Tap ✓ DONE

☞ Go to the home screen ❀²

In the *Tips* at the end of this chapter you will find information about adding and deleting fields. You can also read how to delete a contact.

4.3 Calendar

In the *Calendar* app you can keep a list of your appointments or upcoming activities. This is how you open the app:

☞ If necessary, tap ⚏

☞ Tap Calendar

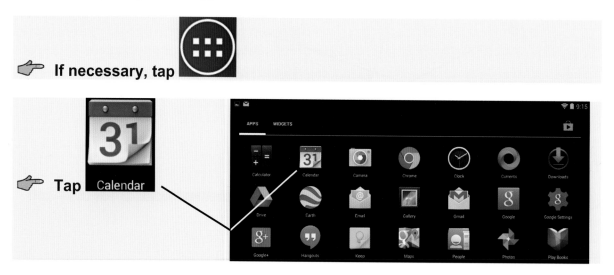

💡 Tip

Other calendar events
If you have previously added calendar events to your *Google* account on another device, such as a mobile phone, they will automatically be synchronized and displayed on your tablet too, if an Internet connection is available.

The calendar will be opened with a display of the current week.

If you have selected a date other than the current day, you can use the 30 **TODAY** button to return to today's events:

If you have signed in to multiple *Google* accounts on your tablet, you can select the calendars you want to view:

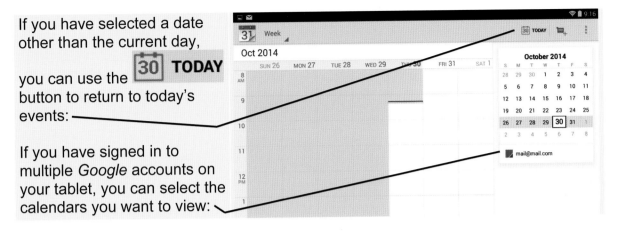

You can display the calendar a week at a time, month at a time, or a full year. This is how you view an entire month:

☞ **If necessary, tap**

Week

☞ **Tap Month**

You will see a view of the full month:

To go to the next month:

☞ **Drag upwards over the screen, until you see the next month**

✚ **HELP! I do not see the next month.**

If you do not see the next month:

☞ **Tap the screen and swipe from right to left or from left to right**

The next month will be displayed:

4.4 Adding an Event

Here is how you add an event to your calendar. You start by selecting the day of the event:

☞ **Tap the desired day**

You will see the week view:

☞ **Tap**

Or:

☞ **Tap** ➕

You can give a name for this event:

☞ **Tap** Event name

Type a name, for example: Tennis lesson

Add a location too:

☞ **Tap** Location

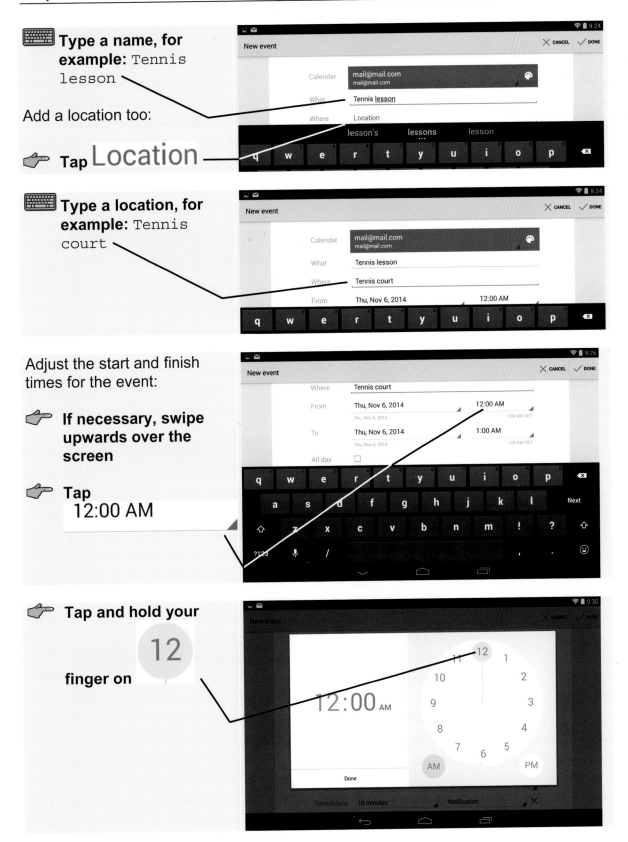

Type a location, for example: Tennis court

Adjust the start and finish times for the event:

☞ **If necessary, swipe upwards over the screen**

☞ **Tap** 12:00 AM

☞ **Tap and hold your** 12 **finger on** 12:00 AM

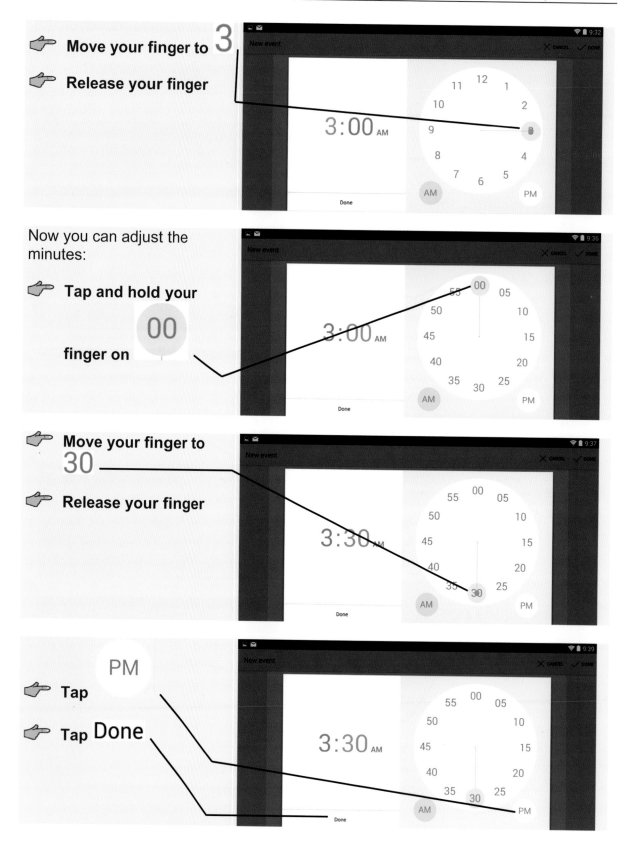

☞ **Move your finger to** 3

☞ **Release your finger**

Now you can adjust the minutes:

☞ **Tap and hold your** 00 **finger on**

☞ **Move your finger to** 30

☞ **Release your finger**

☞ **Tap** PM

☞ **Tap** Done

The end time for the event is automatically adjusted to one hour later: ———

If this is not correct, you can adjust it the same way you did for the start time of the event.

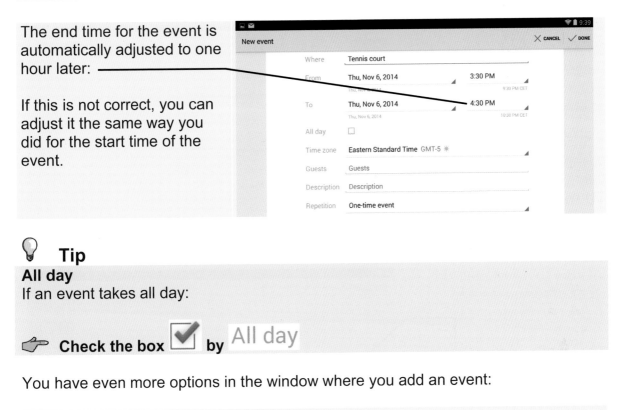

Tip

All day
If an event takes all day:

☞ **Check the box** ✅ **by** All day

You have even more options in the window where you add an event:

☞ If necessary, swipe upwards over the screen

You can add names of guests, and a description for the event: ———

By Repetition you can set up a repeating event, and enter the details of how often it will occur. By default, the **One-time event** option is selected: ———

By Reminders you can set up whether you want to receive a reminder for this event, by way of a notification or an email:

You can choose how far in advance you want to receive the reminder. By default, the **10 minutes** option is selected:

In order to select multiple types of reminders, tap Add reminder:

The last two options can be used by shared calendars:

More information about sharing calendars can be found at the end of this chapter.

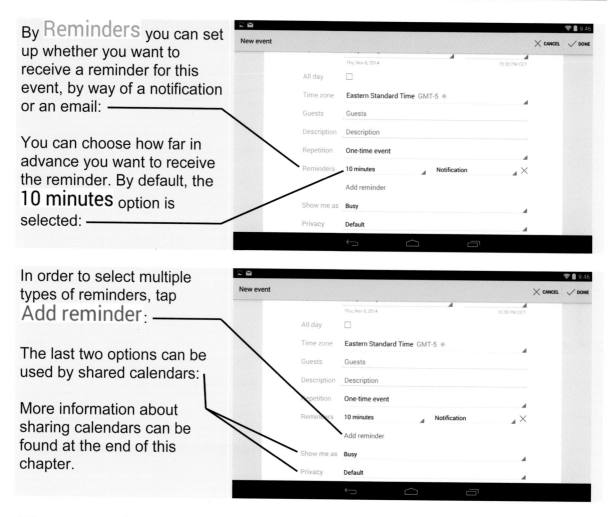

When you are done entering the information for this event:

☞ Tap ✓ **DONE**

You will see the event in your calendar:

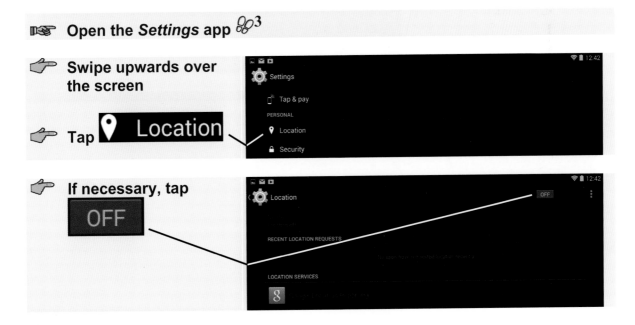

☞ **Go to the home screen** 👣²

In the *Tips* at the end of this chapter you can read how to edit and delete an event.

4.5 Maps

The *Maps* app lets you search for locations and get directions on how to travel to them. Before you start using this app, you will need to make sure your location settings are enabled (turned on). To view these settings:

☞ **Open the *Settings* app** 👣³

👉 **Swipe upwards over the screen**

👉 **Tap 📍 Location**

👉 **If necessary, tap OFF**

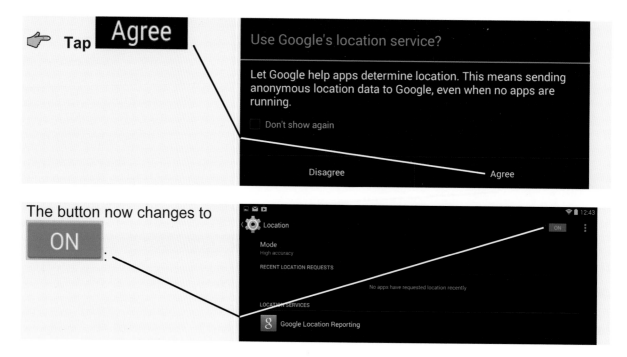

☞ **Tap** **Agree**

Use Google's location service?

Let Google help apps determine location. This means sending anonymous location data to Google, even when no apps are running.

☐ Don't show again

Disagree   Agree

The button now changes to **ON** :

Location
Mode
High accuracy
RECENT LOCATION REQUESTS
No apps have requested location recently
LOCATION SERVICES
g Google Location Reporting

The location services for your tablet are now enabled. For *Google* apps, there are other location settings that can be adjusted separately:

☞ **Tap** [g Google Location Rep]

Location
Mode
High accuracy
RECENT LOCATION REQUESTS
No apps have requested location recently
LOCATION SERVICES
g Google Location Reporting

If the location reporting for *Google* apps has not been enabled, you will see **Location Reporting** Off for this device :

In that case:

☞ **Tap** **Location Reporting** Off for this device

← Google location settings

MAIL@MAIL.COM

Location Reporting
Off for this device

Location History
Off

👉 **Tap** OFF

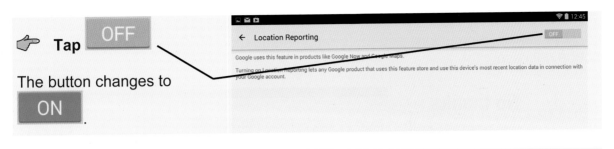

The button changes to

ON .

👉 **Go to the home screen** ᐟᐟ**2**

If you do not want any apps to have access to your location, you can disable these services again, once you have finished this section about working with the *Maps* app.

This is how you open the *Maps* app:

👉 **If necessary, tap**

You will see an apps overview. Not all of the apps may fit onto a single screen. In that case you may need to go to the next screen to find the *Maps* app:

👉 **If necessary, swipe from right to left over the screen**

👉 **Tap** Maps

If you are using the *Maps* app for the first time, you may see this screen:

👉 **If necessary, tap**
Accept & continue

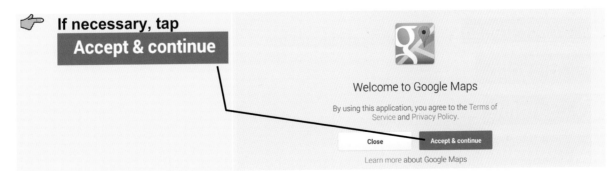

You will be asked if you want to allow *Google* to store your location data in order to improve search suggestions and route recommendations in *Google Maps*. This will not be necessary for now:

☞ **Tap** **No thanks**

If you want to change this setting at a later date, you do this by adjusting a location setting in *Google Maps*. Tap **Location History** by Off to turn Location History on.

You will see your current location on your tablet, with an accuracy of up to 164 feet (50 meters):

Please note: you will see a different location on your own screen.

Open the menu:

☞ **Tap**

This is the information you can add to the map:

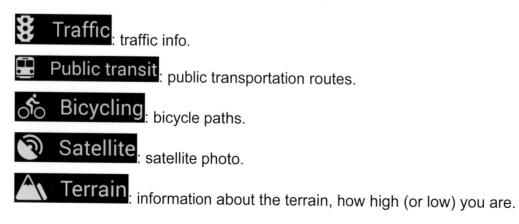

Traffic: traffic info.

Public transit: public transportation routes.

Bicycling: bicycle paths.

Satellite: satellite photo.

Terrain: information about the terrain, how high (or low) you are.

The 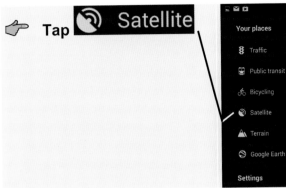 option will bring you to the *Play Store*, where you can download the *Google Earth* app if desired.

👉 **Tap**

You will see a satellite photo of your current location:

💡 **Tip**

Zoom in and out
Spread or pinch two fingers together, in order to zoom in or out.

💡 **Tip**

Turn off or disable satellite view
If you no longer want to view a location in *Satellite* view:

👉 **Tap**

👉 **Tap**

4.6 Finding a Location

Not only can you use *Maps* to search for someone's address, you can also use it to find a well-known location or point of interest:

☞ **Tap** 🔍 Search

⌨ **Type:** mount rushmore

☞ **Tap** 🔍

The location has been found:

☞ **Tap**

Mount Rushmore
National Memorial
4.4 ★★★★★ 282 reviews
Iconic presidential sculpture on a
peak
5:00 AM - 11:00 PM

If you want, you can take an even closer look at the location. In *Maps* you can use the *Street View* option, once you have found a certain location:

☞ **Tap**

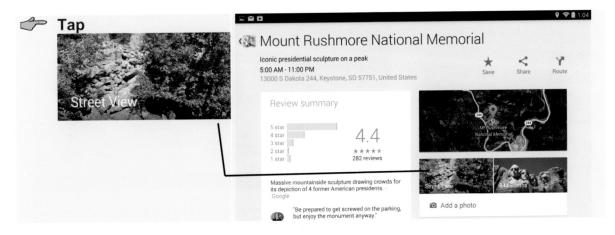

The location will be opened in *Street View*:

You may not see the famous faces right away. The image may have been turned towards another direction. But you can turn the image around yourself:

☞ **If necessary, swipe across the screen from top to bottom (and/or from left to right), until you see the sculptured faces**

You can zoom in on a face:

☞ **Move your thumb and index finger away from**

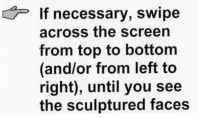

each other

You will see that you have zoomed in:

You can also use the white arrows to move around on the screen:

👉 **Tap**

You will see that the image has moved a bit:

To go back to the map view:

👉 **Tap**  **twice**

💡 **Tip**

Alternate way of opening *Street View*
There is another way of viewing a location in *Street View*:

👉 **Place your finger on the street you want to view**

The address will be determined. Now you can open *Street View* for this location:

👉 **Tap the location, for example**   333-399 Park Rd
Parsippany, NJ 07054

👉 **Tap**

Tip

Extra information

After a specific location has been found, you can see more information about it, for instance, the address, phone number, website, reviews from previous visitors and photos:

4.7 Planning a Trip

Once you have found a desired location, you can get directions to it, starting from your current location or another starting point. You do that like this:

☞ **Tap** Route

You can choose specific directions for travelling by car, using public transportion, cycling, or walking:

You can reverse the start and end points:

Enter a starting point:

☞ **Tap**
   Choose starting point...

Or start from your current
location:

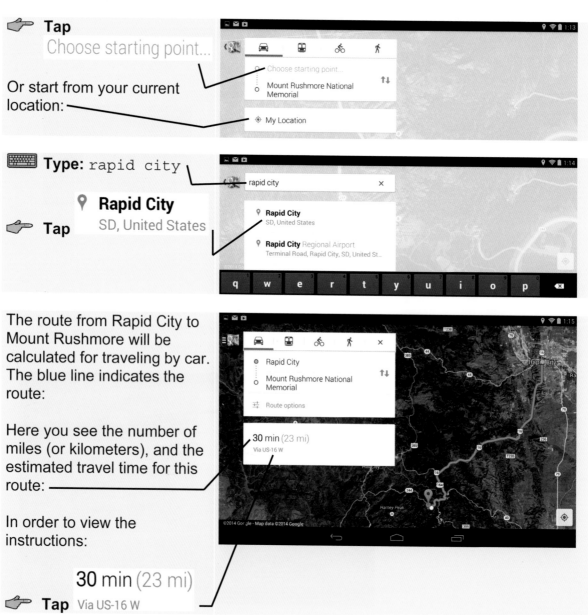

Type: rapid city

   📍 **Rapid City**
      SD, United States

☞ **Tap**

The route from Rapid City to
Mount Rushmore will be
calculated for traveling by car.
The blue line indicates the
route:

Here you see the number of
miles (or kilometers), and the
estimated travel time for this
route:

In order to view the
instructions:

   30 min (23 mi)

☞ **Tap** Via US-16 W

You will see the instructions:

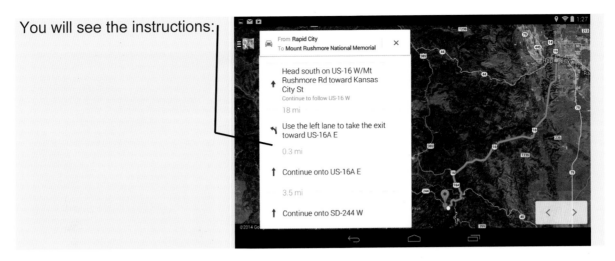

By tapping the instructions you can display parts of the route:

☞ **Tap**

↰ Use the left lane to toward US-16A E

You will see a part of the route:

You can follow the route step-by-step by constantly tapping the next instruction. For now this is not necessary.

This is how you display the full route again:

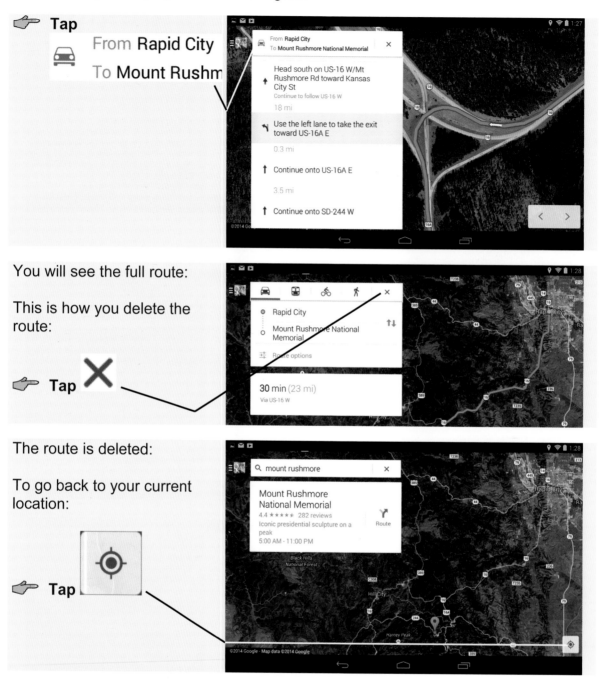

☞ **Tap**

🚗 From **Rapid City**

To **Mount Rushm**

You will see the full route:

This is how you delete the route:

☞ **Tap** ✗

The route is deleted:

To go back to your current location:

☞ **Tap** ⊙

Now you see your current location again.

☞ **Go to the home screen** 👣²

☞ **If desired, disable (turn off) the location services** 👣⁷

4.8 Google Search

The *Google Search* app provides all the search functionality you will need on your tablet. To open *Google Search*:

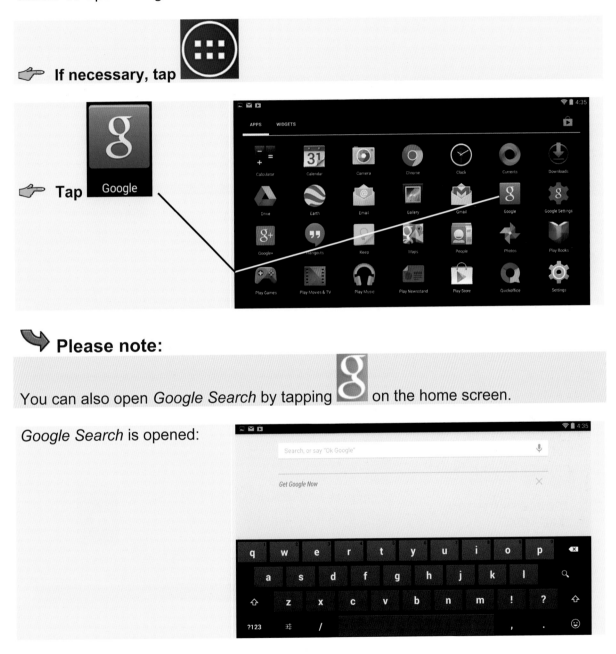

☞ **If necessary, tap**

☞ **Tap** Google

🖐 **Please note:**

You can also open *Google Search* by tapping on the home screen.

Google Search is opened:

 HELP! I see a different window.

If you see a screen with information about *Google Now*, this is what you do:

👉 **Tap** NEXT

On the next screen, on the bottom-left hand:

👉 **Tap** No, maybe later.

You can read more information about *Google Now* in the *Tips* at the end of this chapter.

⌨ **Type:** m

👉 **Tap** 🔍

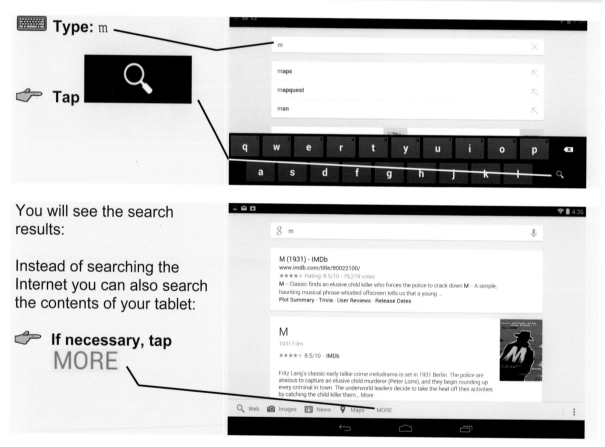

You will see the search results:

Instead of searching the Internet you can also search the contents of your tablet:

👉 **If necessary, tap** MORE

☞ **Tap** ▭ Tablet

M
1931 Film
★★★★★ 8.5/10 · IMDb

Fritz Lang's classic early talkie crime melodrama is set in 1931 Berlin. The police are anxious to capture an elusive child murderer (Peter Lorre), and they begin rounding up every criminal in town. The underworld leaders decide to take the heat off their activities by catching the child killer them... More

Q Web | 📷 Images | 📰 News | 📍 Maps | 🛍 Shopping | 📹 Videos | 📚 Books | ⊞ Applications | ▭ Tablet | ⋮

You will see the search results:

In this example you see a contact listed, among other items:

8 m

Apps   3

Maps   Play Movies & TV

Play Music

Contacts   1

Richard Miller

Q Web | 📷 Images | 📰 News | 📍 Maps | 🛍 Shopping | 📹 Videos | 📚 Books | ⊞ Applications | ▭ Tablet | ⋮

☞ **Go to the home screen** 👣²

💡 **Tip**

Settings for the Google Search app
You can determine which other apps the *Google Search* app is allowed to search:

⋮

☞ **Tap** ⋮

☞ **Tap** Settings

8 m

Apps   3

Maps   Play Movies & TV

Play Music

Contacts   1

Richard Miller

Settings
Send feedback
Help

Q Web | 📷 Images | 📰 News | 📍 Maps | 🛍 Shopping | 📹 Videos | 📚 Books | ⊞ Applications | ▭ Tablet | ⋮

- Continue on the next page -

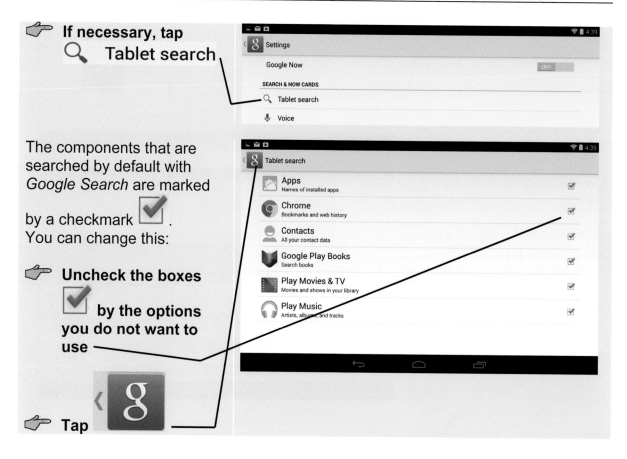

If necessary, tap
🔍 Tablet search

The components that are
searched by default with
Google Search are marked

by a checkmark ✔️ .
You can change this:

Uncheck the boxes
✔️ by the options
you do not want to
use

Tap

4.9 Closing an App

By this point, you have begun using a number of different apps on your tablet. Most
of the time after finishing your work, you have returned to the home screen. When
you do this, some apps may not be shut down and will remain active in the
background. This is usually not a problem, since your tablet hardly consumes any
energy in sleep mode. The big advantage of doing this is that you can immediately
resume working when you re-open the app.

Nevertheless, it is possible to close an app, if you want. You do that as follows:

Tap

You will see the recently used apps:

👉 **Place your finger on the app you want to close**

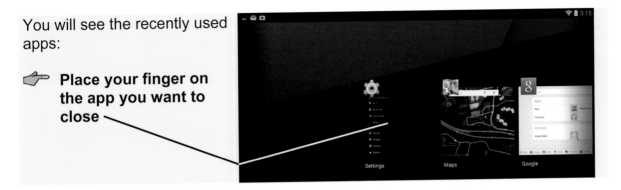

After a while you will see a menu:

👉 **Tap**

Remove from list

The app will be closed.

There is also another way of closing an app:

👉 **Drag the app upwards**

The app will be closed.

☞ **Go to the home screen** 👣²

☞ **If desired, lock or turn off the tablet** 👣⁴

In this chapter you have become acquainted with some of the default apps already installed on your tablet. In the *Tips* at the end of this chapter you will find a list of apps and their brief descriptions that have not been discussed at length in this book.

4.10 Background Information

Dictionary

Album	The name of the folder that contains the photos you have made with your tablet, or the photos stored on your tablet by saving them from an email attachment or website.
Field	An item of data you enter for each contact. *First name* and *Postal code* are examples of fields.
Google Calendar	One of *Google's* free online applications. It lets you keep track of important events and activities. It requires a *Google* account.
Google Maps	An app that lets you look up an address, find a location, view satellite photos, and get different types of travel directions.
Google Now	An extension of *Google Search*. *Google Now* provides additional information that is tailored to the user.
Google Search	The app for searching the Internet or the contents of your tablet.
Label	The name of a field.
Outlook	An email application, part of the *Microsoft Office* suite.
People	An app for managing and maintaining contact information. You can sync contacts across devices using your *Google* account.
Street View	A technology featured in *Google Maps* that allows you to view street-level imagery of a particular location.
Synchronize	Literally: make even. Synchronizing data between two or more devices. Syncing on your *Android* tablet can be enabled or disabled for the various *Google* services that you use.
Windows Live Mail	An email application.

Source: User manual Polaroid tablet, Wikipedia

4.11 Tips

Tip

Add a field

This is how you re-insert a deleted field or add an extra field in the *People* app:

☞ **Open the *People* app** 👣8

👉 **Tap the desired contact**

👉 **Tap**

👉 **Swipe upwards over the screen**

👉 **By the desired field, tap Add new**

Now you can enter the information in the new field and save it.

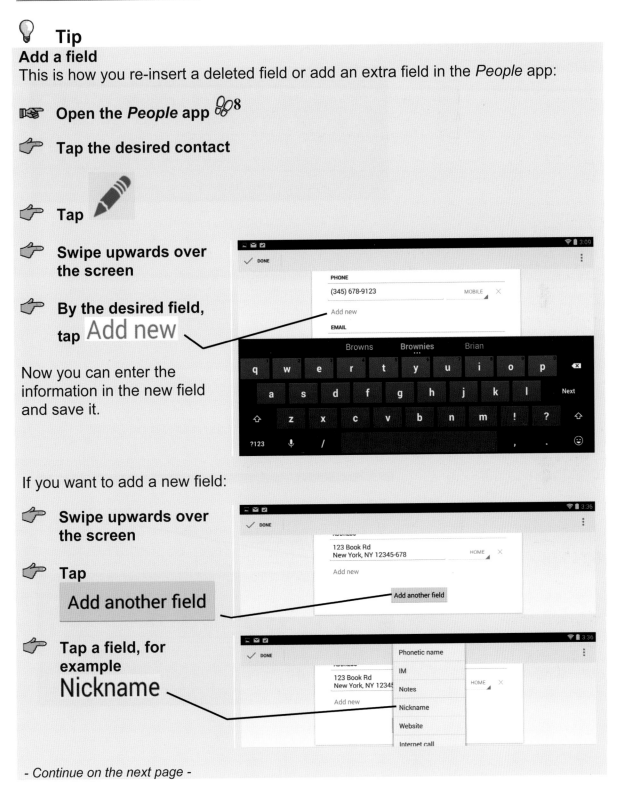

If you want to add a new field:

👉 **Swipe upwards over the screen**

👉 **Tap** Add another field

👉 **Tap a field, for example** Nickname

- Continue on the next page -

The field has been added to the contact data: ──────

Now you can edit the contact data further and save it when you are done.

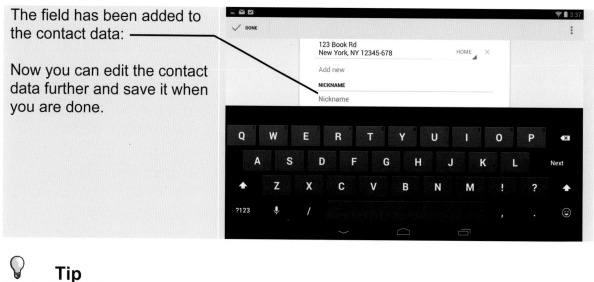

💡 Tip

Delete a field

If you want to completely delete a superfluous field from the contact data in the _People_ app, you do not need to delete the data first:

☞ **Open the _People_ app** 👣8

☞ **Tap the desired contact**

☞ **Tap** 🖊️

By the field you want to delete:

☞ **Tap** ✕

☞ **Tap** ✓ **DONE**

💡 **Tip**

Delete a contact

This is how to permanently delete a contact:

👉 **Open the *People* app** 👣 8

👉 **Tap the desired contact**

👉 **Tap** ■

👉 **Tap Delete**

You will need to confirm this action:

👉 **Tap OK**

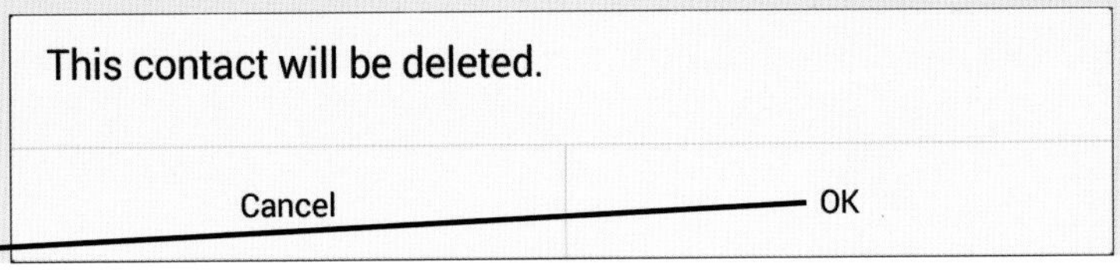

This contact will be deleted.	
Cancel	OK

💡 **Tip**

Find a contact

If you have many contacts stored in the *People* app, it becomes harder to find a specific name. Fortunately, this app also has a useful search feature:

👉 **Open the *People* app** 👣 8

👉 **Tap** 🔍

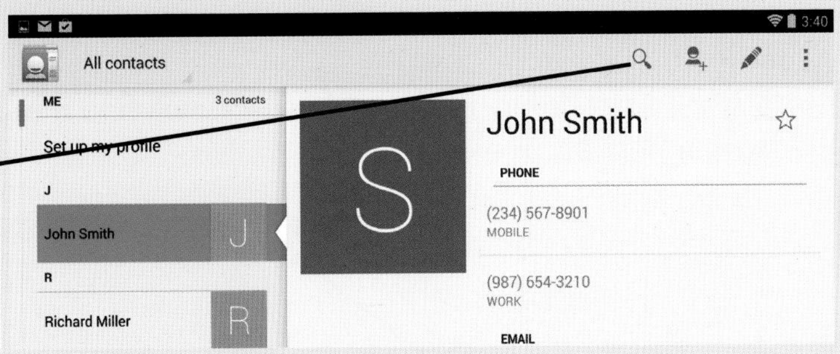

- Continue on the next page -

Type the first letter of the first or last name

In this example, a single contact has been found. To view the information for this contact:

☞ **Tap the contact**

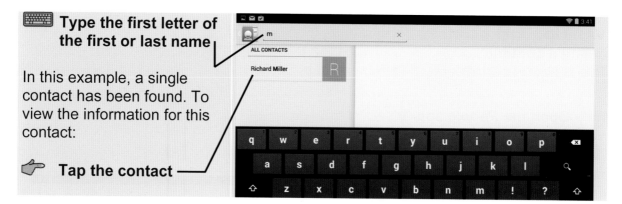

💡 **Tip**

Add a photo

If you have a photo of a contact stored on your tablet, you can add it to the contact information. In *Chapter 6 Photos and Video* you can read how to transfer photos to your tablet. This is how you add an existing photo to the contact's data:

☞ **Open the *People* app** 🐾[8]

☞ **Tap the desired contact**

☞ **Tap** 🖊

☞ **Tap** 👤

☞ **Tap**
Choose photo from Galle

If the photo has recently been added, you will find it in the *Recent* location. Otherwise select another location:

☞ **If necessary, tap**
☰ 🕐 **Recent**

- Continue on the next page -

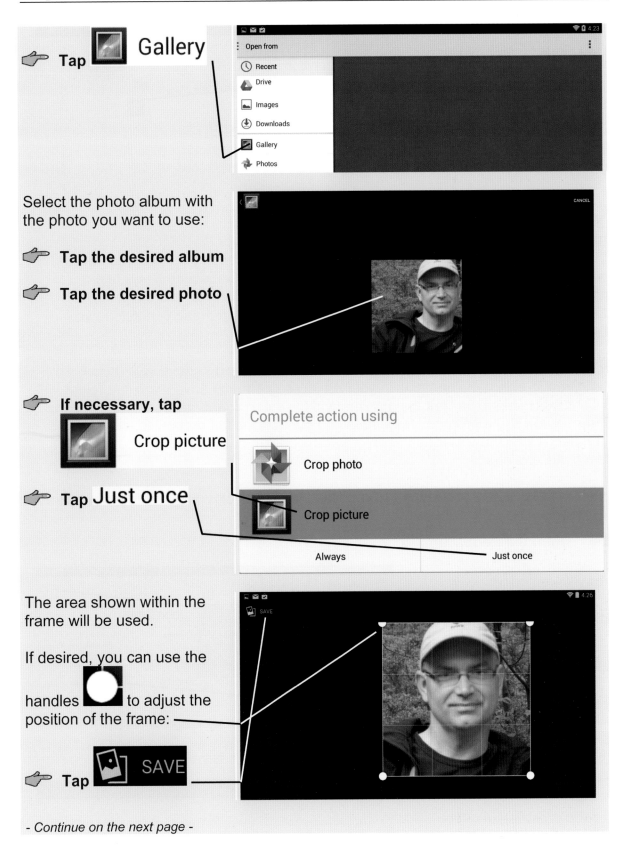

☞ **Tap** Gallery

Select the photo album with the photo you want to use:

☞ **Tap the desired album**

☞ **Tap the desired photo**

☞ **If necessary, tap** Crop picture

☞ **Tap Just once**

The area shown within the frame will be used.

If desired, you can use the handles to adjust the position of the frame:

☞ **Tap** SAVE

- Continue on the next page -

The photo has been added to the contact information:

👉 **Tap** ✓ **DONE**

Google contact	
John Smith	
Add organization	
PHONE	
(234) 567-8901	MOBILE ✕
(987) 654-3210	WORK ✕

💡 **Tip**

Import contacts

The contacts you store in your *Google* account will automatically be synchronized with all the devices on which you use this same *Google* account. If you use a different program on your computer to manage your contacts, such as *Microsoft Outlook* or *Windows Live Mail*, you may be able to import these contacts to your tablet.

If you want to import contacts to your tablet, you will need to have vCard files. You will need to export the contacts in your email program and save them in a folder with vCard files. These are files that use the .vcf file extension. If necessary consult the help section of the program you use to find out information on how to export contacts. Once the folder has been created, you can copy it to your tablet with *Windows Explorer*.

After copying the folder with the vCard files to your tablet, you proceed as follows:

👉 **Open the *People* app** 🦶⁸

👉 **Tap** ⬛

👉 **Tap Import/export**

All contacts		John Smith
ME — 3 contacts		Share
Set up my profile		Delete
J		Place on Home screen
John Smith	J	Contacts to display
R		Import/export
Richard Miller	R	Accounts
S		Settings
Sophia Brown	S	Help

PHONE (234) 567-8901 MOBILE / (987) 654-3210 HOME
EMAIL name@provider.com HOME
ADDRESS 123 Book Rd New York, NY 12345-678

- Continue on the next page -

👉 **Tap**
Import from storage

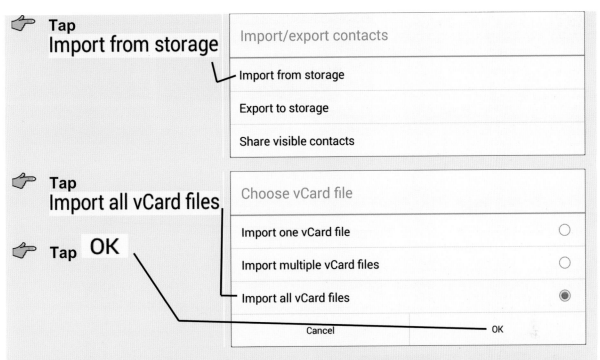

Import/export contacts

Import from storage

Export to storage

Share visible contacts

👉 **Tap**
Import all vCard files

👉 **Tap** **OK**

Choose vCard file

Import one vCard file ◯

Import multiple vCard files ◯

Import all vCard files ⦿

Cancel   OK

The contacts will be imported to your tablet. Keep in mind that some contact data fields may not be imported to the data on your tablet.

💡 **Tip**
Edit or delete an event
If an event needs to be changed or has been canceled, you can change it in the *Calendar* app:

👉 **If necessary, tap the date**

👉 **Tap the event**

👉 **Tap**

You will see the window in which you had entered the original event. You can edit the description, location, date, or time of the event. After you have finished editing:

👉 **Tap** ✓ **DONE**

- Continue on the next page -

If you want to delete the event:

☞ **Tap**

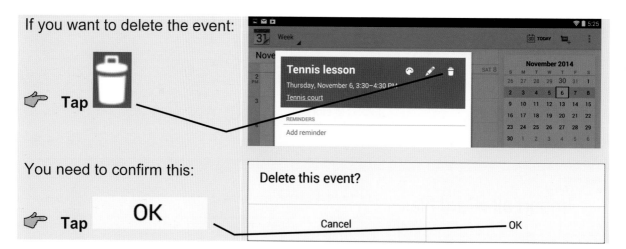

You need to confirm this:

Delete this event?

☞ **Tap** **OK**

Cancel   OK

💡 **Tip**

Traffic information

In the *Maps* app you can display the current traffic information:

☞ **Tap** [Maps icon], [Traffic icon] Traffic

The traffic flow will be displayed in a color:

Green: the traffic flows smoothly at the normal speed.

Yellow: the traffic moves slower than the speed limit.

Red: the traffic is congested, and moves very slowly.

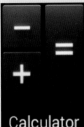

Tip

Other apps

Your tablet contains many more apps than can be discussed in this book. Below you will find a brief description of some of the other apps that may be included on your tablet. The apps that are discussed in the following chapters are not included here.

Calculator

Calculator.

Clock

With this app you can view the current date and time, set an alarm, and view the time in other parts of the world. You can also use this app as a timer and a stopwatch.

Currents

An app that presents current news in a magazine-like format.

Downloads

This app provides direct access to the folder that contains the files that have been downloaded to the tablet.

Drive

This app allows you to use the storage and synchronization service called *Google Drive*. With *Google Drive* you can store and access your files anywhere and share them with others.

- Continue on the next page -

Earth

With the *Google Earth* app you can find virtually any place in the world. *Google Earth* uses satellite and aerial imagery, ocean bathymetry, and other geographic data over the Internet to represent the Earth as a three-dimensional globe. The app has more options available than *Google Maps*, especially in the field of visual material.

Google Settings

In this app you can change a number of settings that are specific to *Google*.

Google+

The social network site provided by *Google* that is comparable to *Facebook*. In order to use this service you need to use your *Google* account and create a profile.

Hangouts

With this app you can conduct video calls and send photos to anyone that has been added to *Hangouts*. In order to use *Hangouts* you need to be connected to the Internet and use a *Google* account. Your contact also needs to have a *Google* account and be a user of *Google Hangouts*.

Keep

An app that allows you to create notes. You can also use this app to save photos, voice memos and receive reminders.

Play Books

An app to read and purchase books.

- Continue on the next page -

Play Games

An app with which you can purchase games, keep scores, and play games with others.

Play Movies & TV

You can use this app to watch movies you have purchased or rented from *Google Play*.

Play Newsstand

An app for reading and viewing news and magazines from free or paid sources, from blogs and newspapers to the *New Yorker* and more.

Quickoffice

An app with which you can view and edit *Microsoft Word*, *Excel*, and *PowerPoint* files. You can also view PDF files with this app.

Voice Search

An app which allows you to use *Google Search* by giving speech commands that contain the search terms or phrases to be used.

YouTube

An app with which you can watch videos on *YouTube*.

Tip

Widgets

Besides apps, your tablet also contains widgets. Widgets are actually small programs, related to apps. You can move widgets to the home screen:

☞ Tap

☞ Tap **WIDGETS**

☞ **Place your finger on a widget, for example Calendar**

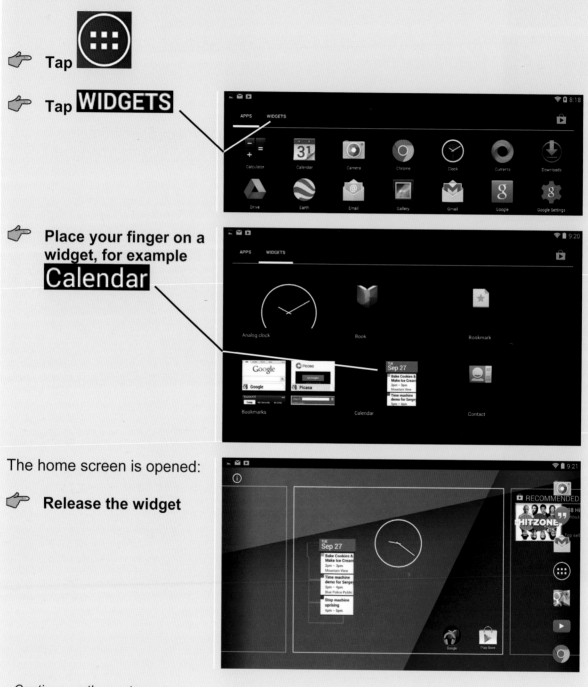

The home screen is opened:

☞ **Release the widget**

- Continue on the next page -

The widget has been moved to your home screen:

In this example you see the *Calendar* widget, showing one event.

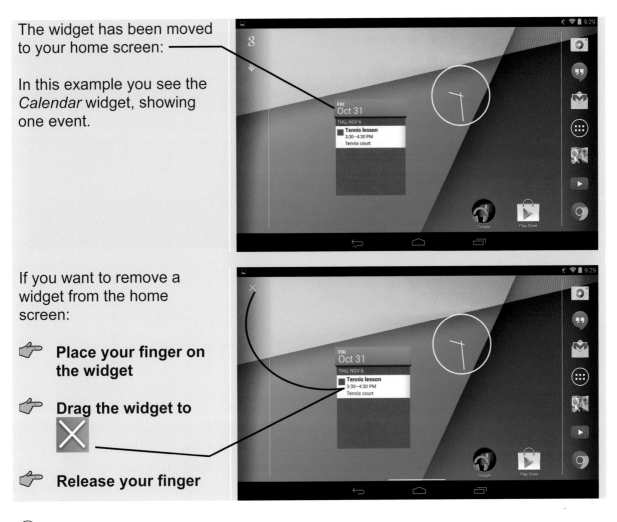

If you want to remove a widget from the home screen:

☞ **Place your finger on the widget**

☞ **Drag the widget to**

☞ **Release your finger**

💡 Tip

Notifications

In the top left-hand corner of the screen you will see a variety of symbols. These are the icons that are used for notifications of email messages, new events in your calendar, and other events, among other things.

Here you see the notification symbols:

☞ **Drag downwards, from the top left-hand corner of the screen**

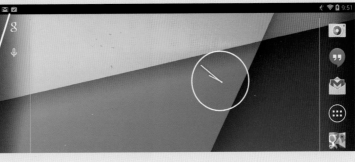

- Continue on the next page -

You will see the notifications:

In order to go to the corresponding app, you tap the icon to the left of the notification:

You can delete a notification by dragging it away to the left or the right.

You can also delete all the notifications at once, by

tapping 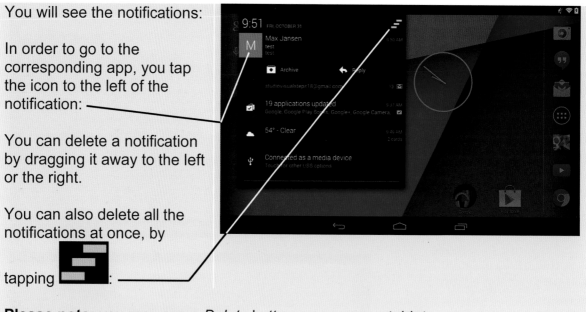 :

Please note: you may see a *Delete* button on your own tablet.

💡 Tip
Disable synchronization
The information in your *Google* account will automatically be synchronized with all the other devices on which you use this *Google* account. This means that the data you have previously added to your account will also be displayed and used on your tablet. If desired, you can disable this function for each individual app:

Please note: depending on your type of tablet, you may not be able to turn off this function.

☞ **Open the *Settings* app** ✌¹

☞ **If necessary, swipe upwards over the screen**

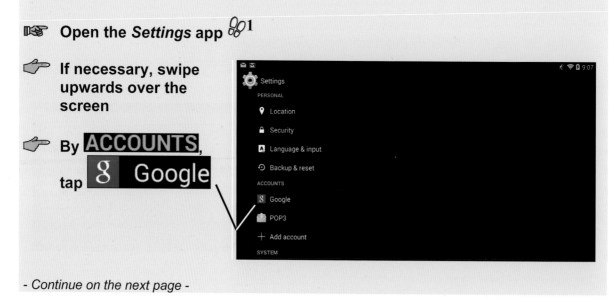

☞ **By ACCOUNTS,**

tap Google

- Continue on the next page -

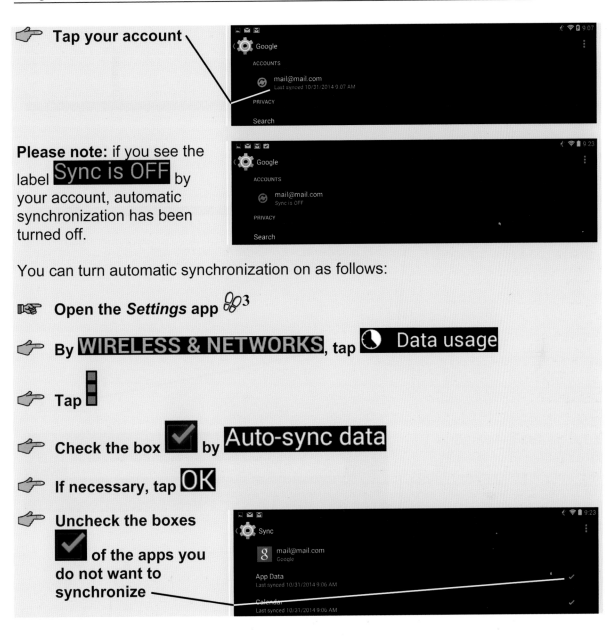

☞ **Tap your account**

Please note: if you see the label Sync is OFF by your account, automatic synchronization has been turned off.

You can turn automatic synchronization on as follows:

☞ **Open the *Settings* app** 🐾³

☞ **By WIRELESS & NETWORKS, tap 🌐 Data usage**

☞ **Tap ▮**

☞ **Check the box ✔ by Auto-sync data**

☞ **If necessary, tap OK**

☞ **Uncheck the boxes ✔ of the apps you do not want to synchronize**

💡 **Tip**

Google Now
Google Now is an extension of the *Google Search* app. You can look upon *Google Now* as a personal assistant. You can receive current information at any given moment, for example, about the weather, the traffic situation, your appointments, and special attractions. *Google Now* uses your personal information for this function, such as location data (provided location services have been enabled), your calendar and your browser history.

- Continue on the next page -

This is how you enable *Google Now*:

☞ **Open the *Google Search* app** 🐾8

👉 **Tap**
Get Google Now

👉 **Tap** YES, I'M IN.

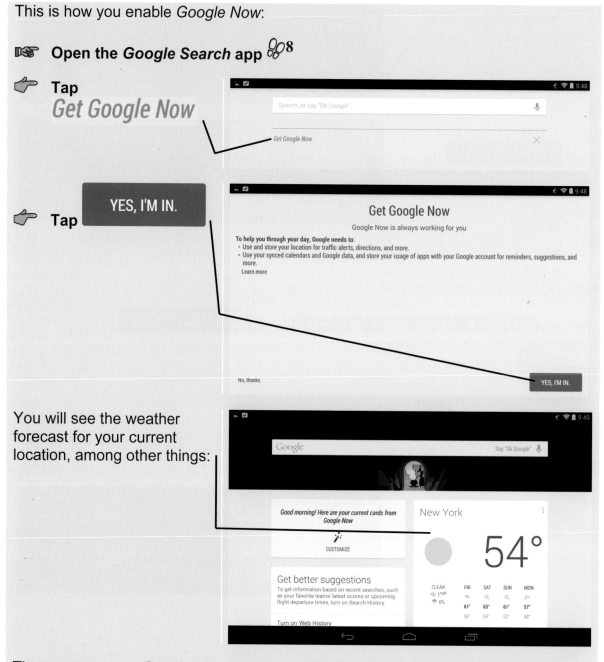

You will see the weather forecast for your current location, among other things:

The more you use *Google Now* and your tablet, the better *Google Now* will be able to inform you about different things.

5. Downloading Apps

In the previous chapters you have become acquainted with some of the standard apps installed on your tablet. In the *Play Store* app there are literally thousands of apps that can be purchased or acquired for free. New apps can provide additional productivity, help you to accomplish daily tasks quickly, and give you hours of entertainment.

There are far too many apps to list all of them in this book. There are apps for newspapers and magazines, weather forecasts, games, recipes, and sports results. You will surely find something that interests you.

In this chapter you will learn how to download a free app from the *Play Store* app. If you want to purchase an app, you can use a *Google Play Gift Card* to pay for it, or link a credit card to your *Google* account. It only takes a few steps to do this.

Once you have purchased some apps, you can change the order in which they are arranged on the screen of your tablet. You can even create folders for you apps and store related apps in them. You can also delete the apps you no longer want to use.

In this chapter you will learn how to:

- download and install a free app;
- download and install a paid app;
- set up a password for your purchases;
- move apps;
- save apps in a folder;
- delete apps.

Please note:

In order to buy and download apps in the *Play Store* app, you need to have linked a *Google* account to your tablet. If you do not yet have a *Google* account, you can read how to create one in *section 1.7 Creating and Adding a Google Account*.

Please note:

The screens you see on your own tablet may look different from the images in this book. The buttons may also have a different name or look a little different. Always search for a similar button or function. The basic operations will remain the same.

5.1 Downloading a Free App

In the *Play Store* app you will find thousands of free apps. This is how you open the *Play Store* app:

☞ **Unlock or turn on your tablet** 👣¹

☞ **If necessary, tap**

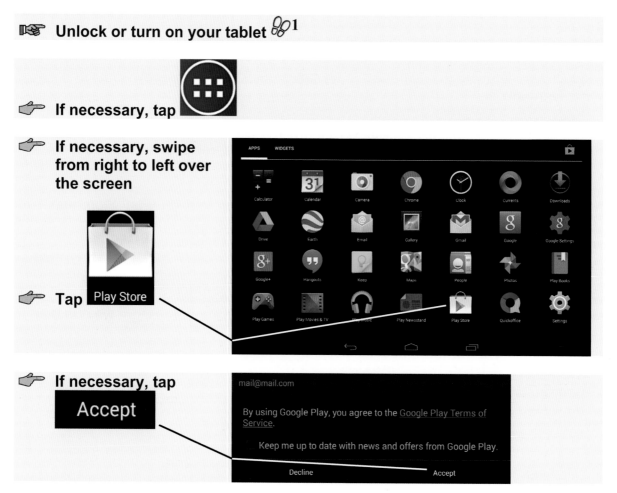

☞ **If necessary, swipe from right to left over the screen**

☞ **Tap** Play Store

☞ **If necessary, tap** Accept

The *Play Store* app will be opened. You will be signed in automatically with your *Google* account.

💡 Tip

Multiple accounts
If your tablet is linked to multiple *Google* accounts, you can decide which account is to be used in the *Play Store* app. Tap ▬ in the top-left corner of your screen, tap ▼ by the account name shown and then tap the account name that will be used for the *Play Store* app.

Besides apps you can also download games, music, books, movies, and magazines and newspapers:

To download an app:

☞ **Tap** APPS

You will see the homepage, where the newest apps are highlighted:

☞ **Tap** CATEGORIES

You will see a list with categories of the available apps:

☞ **Swipe upwards over the left side of the screen**

☞ **Tap** Weather

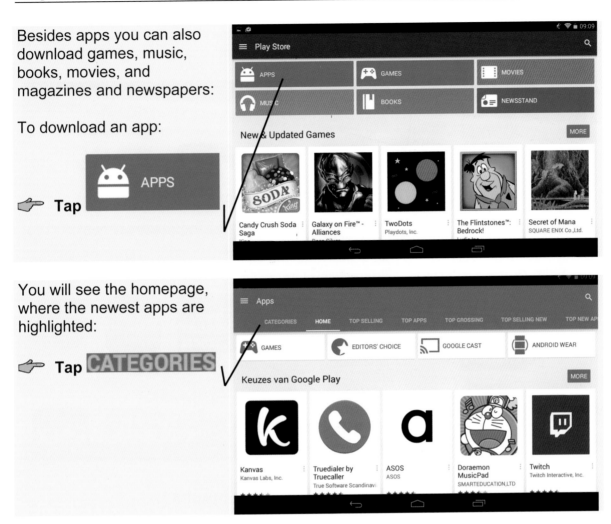

You will see a page with best-selling apps in the *Weather* category. The paid apps are shown first. To go to the most popular free apps in the same category:

Tap **TOP APPS**

Look for the free app called *The Weather Channel* for example:

If necessary, swipe upwards over the screen

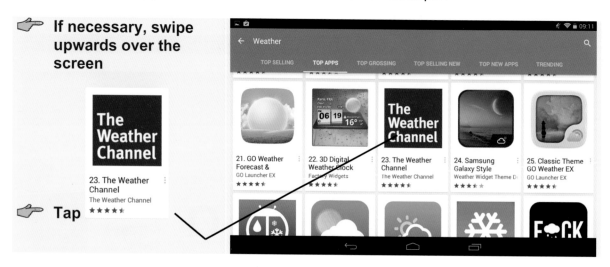

Tap

HELP! I do not see the The Weather Channel app.

If you cannot find the *The Weather Channel* app, you can search for it using the search box. On page 151 you can read how to do this.

A new window is opened with all kinds of information about this app. If you want to download the app:

Tap **INSTALL**

You will see the authorizations required in order for the app to perform correctly on your tablet. You will need to accept these conditions:

☞ **Tap**

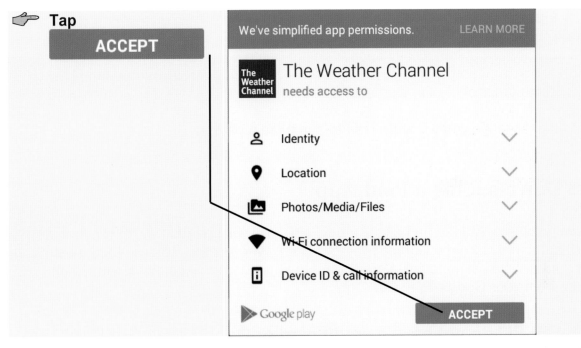

The app will be installed. Once the installation process has finished, you can open the app right away:

☞ **Tap**

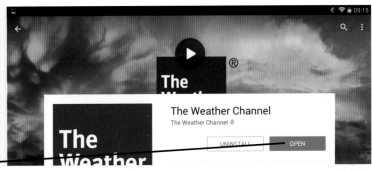

You will see the *The Weather Channel* app:

This app shows you the current temperature, and also lets you know if it is going to rain, and where it will rain.

Go to the home screen ✂²

💡 **Tip**

Managing apps

The new app will automatically appear on the home screen. The app will also be displayed in the apps overview. In *section 5.4 Managing Apps* you can read how to change the order of the apps on your screen.

In the next section you will learn how to purchase a paid app.

5.2 Downloading a Paid App

If you want to download and install a paid app, you will need to pay for it with a credit card or the credit from a *Google Play Gift Card*. When you try to download a paid app, you will be asked to link a credit card to your *Google* account, or redeem the credit from your *Google Play Gift Card*.

✖ **HELP! I do not have a credit card or Google Play Gift Card.**

If you do not have a credit card, you may want to consider purchasing a prepaid credit card. Companies such as www.skrill.com and www.paysafecard.com offer cards for as little as ten dollars, for example. After you have purchased a card, you can 'load' it with the amount you want to use. With a prepaid credit card, you can only pay with the amount that has been deposited on the credit card beforehand. You do not have to enter any personal information or your bank details when paying online, so the risk is much lower. You can purchase a *Google Play Gift Card* online or in stores and redeem the credit on it in the *Play Store* app.

☞ **Open the *Play Store* app** ✂⁸

You previously found an app by looking through the categories. But if you know the name of the app you want to download you can search for it directly:

The page with *The Weather Channel* app information may still be shown:

In the upper-right corner of the screen:

☞ **Tap**

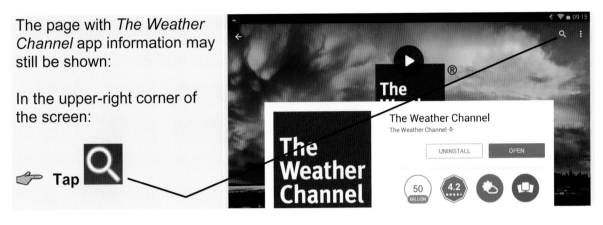

In this example we will search for a Sudoku game:

⌨ **Type:** sudoku

☞ **Tap**

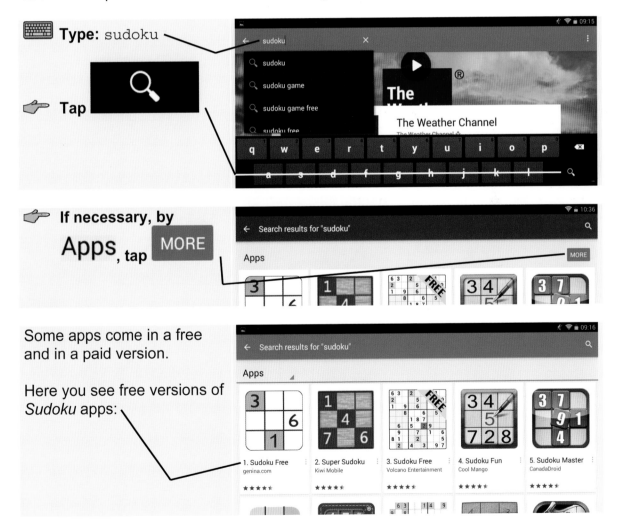

☞ **If necessary, by**

Apps, **tap** MORE

Some apps come in a free and in a paid version.

Here you see free versions of *Sudoku* apps:

This time you will look for the paid version of the app:

👉 **Swipe upwards over the screen**

👉 **Tap**

🖐 **Please note:**

In this section we will be going through the steps needed to purchase an app. You can decide for yourself whether you want to purchase this app. Of course, you do not need to buy the same app as in this example. After ordering an app, you have the option of cancelling the order if that is done within fifteen minutes after placing the order. You can find more information about this topic in the *Tip Cancel an order* on page 155.

In this example, the app we purchase costs 1.99:

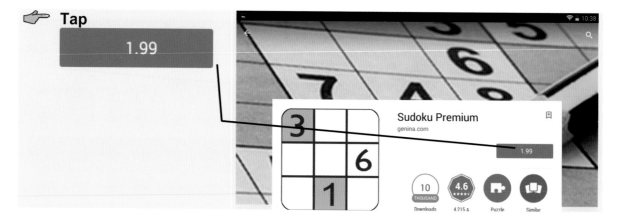

👉 **Tap**

1.99

You will see the window where you need to accept the authorizations again:

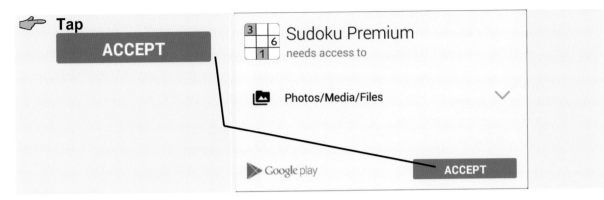

👉 **Tap**

ACCEPT

🐟 **Please note:**

If you have not linked a credit card to your *Google* account or have not activated a *Google Play Gift Card* you will see a few additional screens. You will be asked to enter your credit card information or to enter the code shown on your *Google Play Gift Card*.

Once the information has been entered, you can proceed further with the purchase:

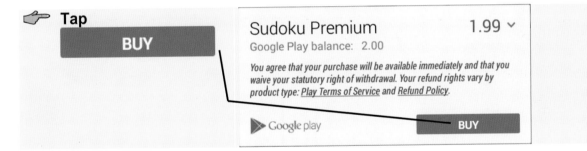

👉 **Tap**

BUY

You may need to confirm this purchase with your *Google* password:

⌨️ **If necessary, type your password**

👉 **If necessary, tap**

CONFIRM

Confirm password
mail@mail.com

Sudoku Premium   **1.99**
Google Play balance: 2.00

•••••••••   ⑦

☐ NEVER ASK ME AGAIN

▶ Google play   **CONFIRM**

Tip

Set up a password for purchases
In *section 5.3 Setting Up a Password for Purchases* you can read how to change the setting for a security password.

You can select one of two options before you are prompted to enter a password again when making a purchase:

☞ **Tap the desired option**

Payment successful

You can choose to be prompted for a password once every 30 minutes for purchases of all forms of digital content, including in-app purchases.

How often would you like to confirm your password for purchases?

EVERY TIME   EVERY 30 MIN

Once the app has been downloaded, you will receive an email from *Google Play*. In the upper-left corner of the screen you will see a notification.

The app has been installed. Go back to the *Play Store* home page:

☞ **Tap** ⬅ **a few times until you see** ☰ **Apps**

☞ **Tap** ☰

☞ **Tap Store home**

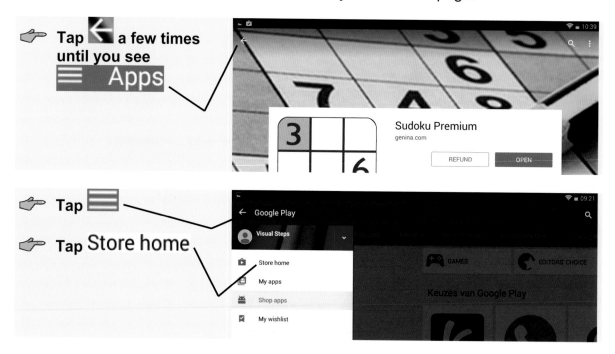

You will see the *Play Store's* home page. You can view the downloaded app later on.

💡 Tip

Cancel an order

You can cancel a purchase within fifteen minutes of ordering. This can be useful if you have made a mistake, or on second thought, do not like the app after all. To start the refund process:

👉 **Open the *Play Store* app** 👣8

To view the installed apps:

👉 **Tap** ☰

👉 **Tap My apps**

👉 **If necessary, swipe upwards over the screen**

👉 **Tap the app**

👉 **Tap**

> REFUND

Please note: after fifteen minutes you will no longer see this button.

👉 **Tap** **Yes**

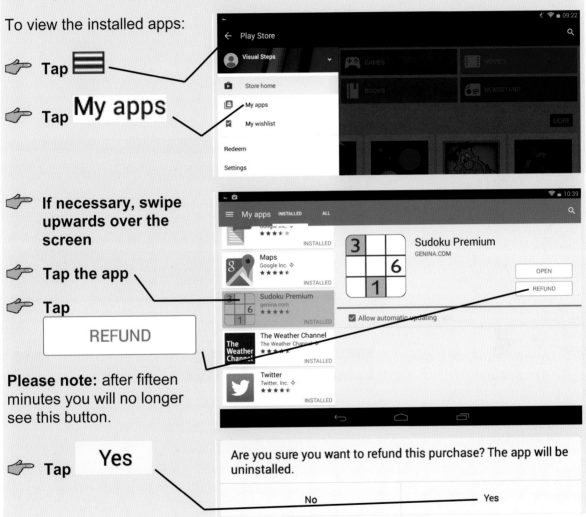

5.3 Setting Up a Password for Purchases

You can prevent unintentional purchases from occurring by enabling password protection. The password protection may already be enabled for all purchases, since that is the default setting. But if it is not enabled, you can adjust the settings for it.

⤵ Please note:

In some games apps, while you play, you can buy fake money to bargain with in the game. You pay for this fake money in regular currency, using your credit card or *Google Play Gift Card*. If you let your children or grandchildren play a game, they might be able to purchase fake money without you noticing it. That is why it is a good idea to set up a password for all your purchases in the *Play Store* app.

You will see the *Play Store's* home page:

☞ Tap ▤

☞ Tap Settings

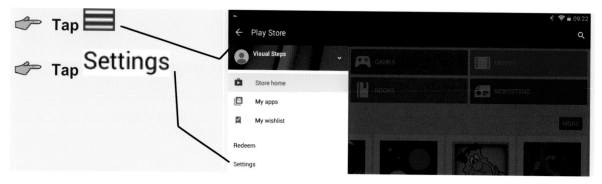

Check if the password has been set:

☞ **Swipe upwards over the screen**

By **Require password for purchases**, you will see the current setting. In this case a password is required every 30 minutes:

To make sure a password is required for all purchases:

☞ **Tap Require password for p**
Every 30 minutes

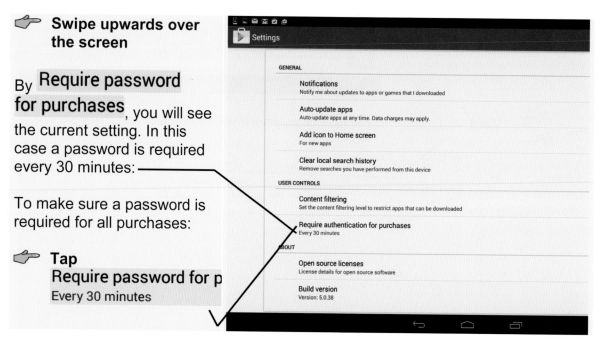

To make sure a password is required for all purchases:

👉 **Tap the radio button** 🔘 **by**
For all purchases through

> Require authentication
>
> For all purchases through Google Play on this device ◯
>
> Every 30 minutes ⦿
>
> Never ◯
>
> Cancel

⌨ **Type the password**

👉 **Tap OK**

> Confirm password
>
> mail@mail.comm
>
> • • • • • • • • •
>
> Forgot password?
>
> Cancel | OK

You will see the new setting:

Go back to the home page:

> USER CONTROLS
>
> **Content filtering**
> Set the content filtering level to restrict apps that can be downloaded
>
> **Require authentication for purchases**
> For all purchases through Google Play on this device
>
> ABOUT
>
> **Open source licenses**
> License details for open source software
>
> **Build version**
> Version: 5.0.38

👉 **Tap** ⬅

From now on you will see a confirmation screen each time you try to purchase an item in the *Play Store* app:

> # Confirm password
> mail@mail.com
>
> • • • • • • • • • ⦰
>
> ☐ NEVER ASK ME AGAIN
>
> ▶ Google play   **CONFIRM**

🖐 **Please note:**

When you download free apps, you will not be asked to enter your password.

👉 **Go to the home screen** 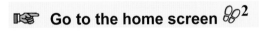²

5.4 Managing Apps

You can change the arrangement of the apps on your screen. You do this by moving them around and rearranging them in whatever order you want.

Please note:

In order to carry out the next few steps, you need to have installed at least two apps. If you have not purchased an app, you can download another free app that interests you, as described in *section 5.1 Downloading a Free App*.

You will see the installed apps on the home screen:

Please note: if you do not see the installed apps on your home screen, they may have been placed on a different page. In that case, swipe from right to left over the screen.

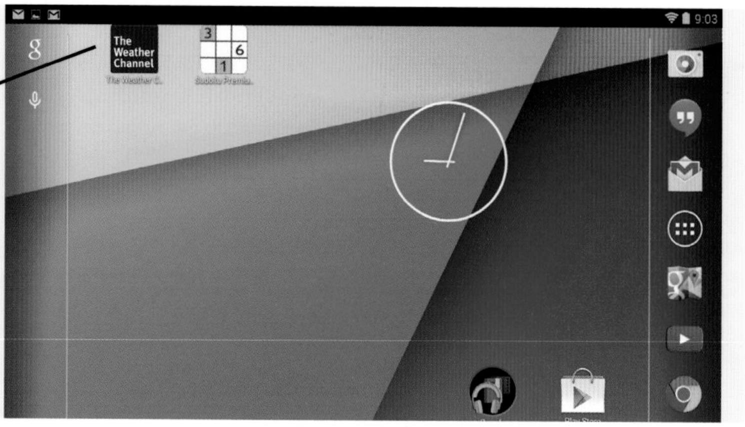

You can arrange the apps any way you want. This is how you move an app:

- **Place and hold your finger on the app**
- **Drag the app to another position**
- **Release it**

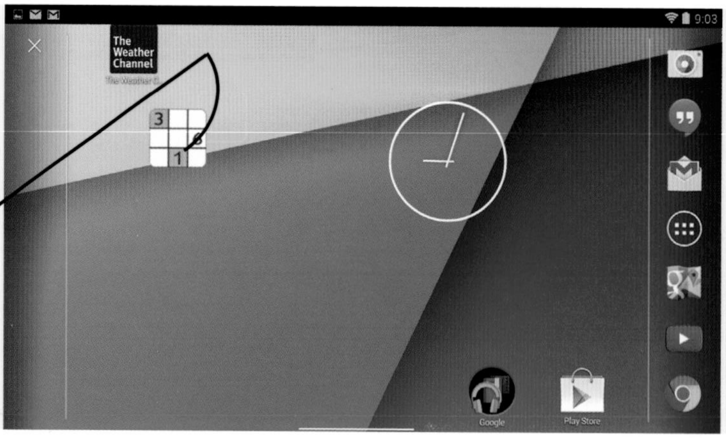

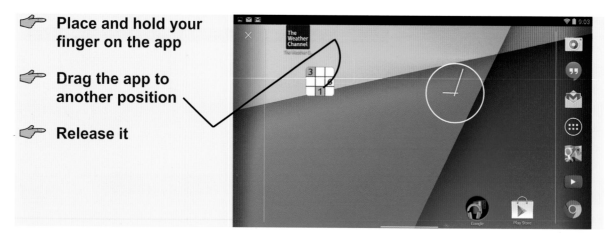

HELP! The search box is in my way.

On some tablets there may be a search bar or box on the home screen. If the new apps are placed behind the *Google Search* box, it may be difficult to select them. In that case, you need to place your finger on the part of the app's icon that appears outside of the search box.

The app has been moved:

You can also move the app to another page. Here is how to do that:

☞ **Press and hold your finger on the app**

☞ **Drag the app to the left border of the screen**

As soon as you see the other page:

☞ **Release your finger**

The app has been moved to the other page:

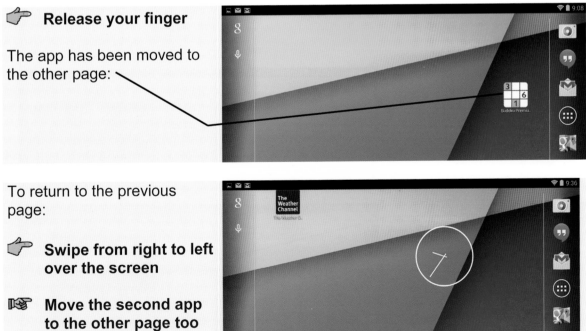

To return to the previous page:

☞ **Swipe from right to left over the screen**

☞ **Move the second app to the other page too** 👣9

You can also store related apps together in the same folder. Here is how to do that:

☞ **Press and hold your finger on an app**

☞ **Drag the app on top of the other app**

When a circle or a frame appears around the other app:

☞ **Release your finger**

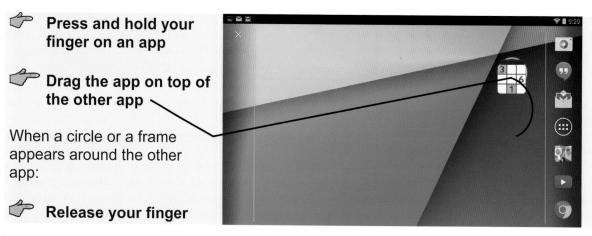

🩹 **HELP! I do not see a circle or frame.**

If you do not see a circle or frame around the app and the app looks as if it has just switched places on the screen, you may be dragging a little too slow. Try to drag a little faster. It takes some practice to drag effectively.

The app is now contained within a folder:

☞ **Tap the folder**

The folder is opened:

You can enter a name for this folder:

☞ **Tap** **Unnamed Folder**

⌨ **Type a name**

☞ **Tap** **Done**

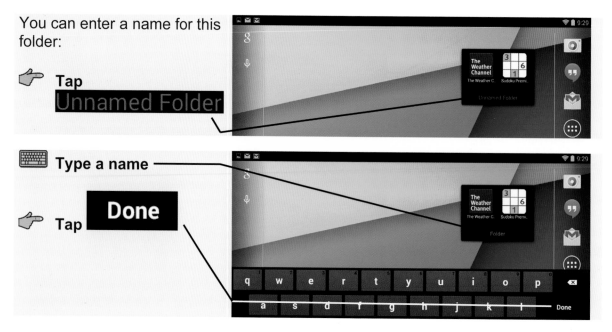

👉 **Tap next to the folder**

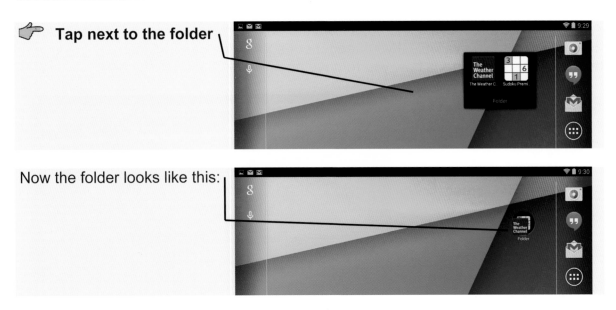

Now the folder looks like this:

You can add more apps to the folder. You do this by dragging the apps to the folder in the same way as described earlier.

If you want to take an app out of the folder (remove it from the folder):

👉 **Tap the folder**

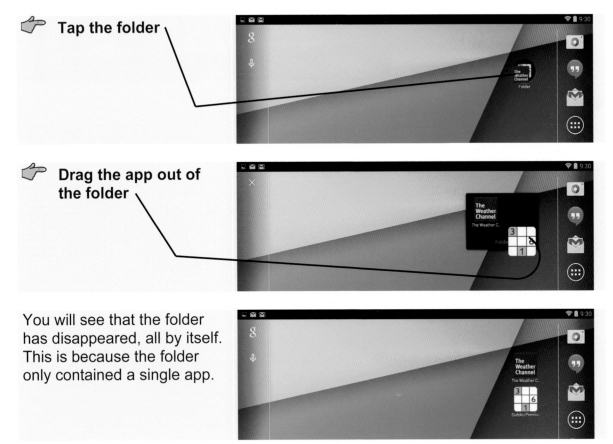

👉 **Drag the app out of the folder**

You will see that the folder has disappeared, all by itself. This is because the folder only contained a single app.

Would you like to remove some apps from the home screen? They will not be deleted and will still remain available if you need them again. You can find them by going to the apps overview. This is how you remove an app from the home screen:

👉 **Press and hold your finger on the desired app**

At the top of the screen, ✕ appears:

👉 **Drag the app to** ✕

👉 **Release your finger**

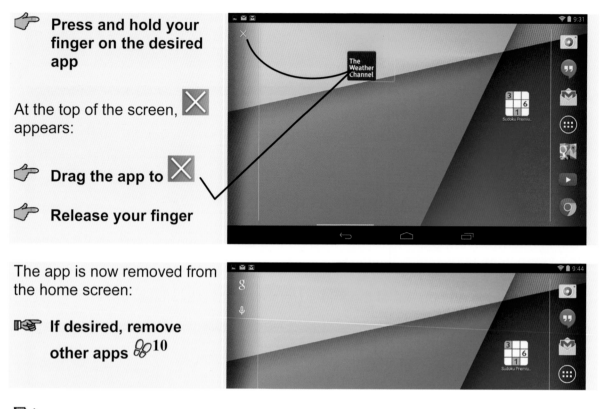

The app is now removed from the home screen:

👉 **If desired, remove other apps** 🦶10

🐾 **Please note:**

When you remove an app from the home screen, you are only removing the link (shortcut) to the app. You are not deleting the app from your tablet. The app can still be found in the apps overview. In the next section we will explain how to completely delete an app from your tablet.

5.5 Deleting an App

If you have downloaded an app that on second thought is a bit disappointing, then you can delete this app through the *Play Store* app.

👉 **Open the *Play Store* app** 🦶8

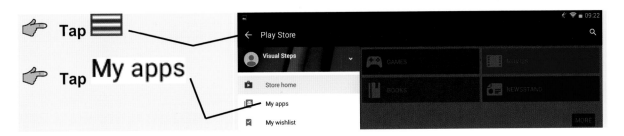

☞ Tap ▤

☞ Tap **My apps**

You will see the list with the installed apps. You can delete the apps you have downloaded from the *Play Store* app:

☞ **If necessary, swipe upwards over the left side of the screen**

☞ **Tap the app**

☞ **Tap**

UNINSTALL

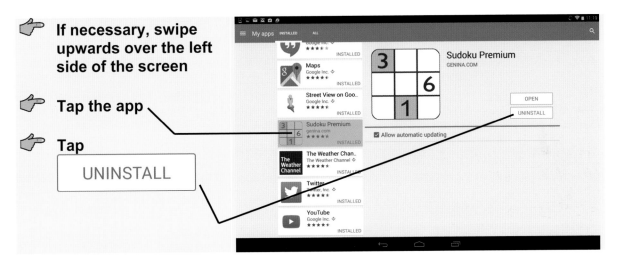

If you really want to delete the app:

☞ Tap **OK**

Do you want to uninstall this app?

Cancel   OK

The app will be deleted from the tablet. You can always re-install an app that you have purchased without the need of purchasing it again. Your *Play Store* purchasing information will remain stored and associated with your *Google* account. See the *Tip Download a paid app once more* at the end of this chapter.

☞ **Go to the home screen** 🦶²

☞ **If desired, lock or turn off the tablet** 🦶⁴

In this chapter you have learned how to download free and paid apps from the *Play Store* app. You have also learned how to arrange apps on your home screen, create folders of apps, and how to delete apps.

5.6 Background Information

Dictionary

App	Short for application, a program for the tablet.
Favorites tray	You can find the favorites tray on the home screen. This allows you to quickly navigate to your apps, books, music, et cetera.
Google account	A combination of an email address and a password. You need to have a *Google* account in order to download apps from the *Play Store* app.
Play Store	An online shop where you can download apps for free or for a fee.

Source: User manual Polaroid tablet

5.7 Tips

Tip
Updating apps
After a while, the apps that are installed on your tablet will be updated. These free updates may be necessary to solve certain problems (often called bug fixes). An update can also contain new functions or additional options, such as a new level in a game app. You can check for updates yourself:

☞ **Open the *Play Store* app** $\%^8$

☞ **Tap** ▬

☞ **Tap** **My apps**

In this example, there are updates available for a few apps:

The standard setting allows apps to be updated automatically. If you do not want this to happen, you can

uncheck the box ☑ by **Allow automatic updating** for each app.

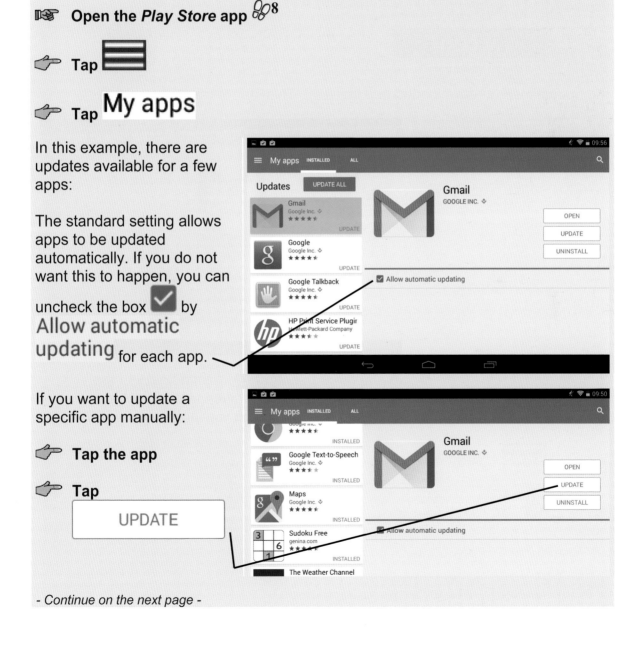

If you want to update a specific app manually:

☞ **Tap the app**

☞ **Tap**

UPDATE

- Continue on the next page -

In order to carry out all the
updates immediately:

☞ **Tap**

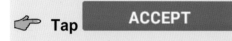

You may see a few extra windows, and may need to agree to the terms:

☞ **Tap** ACCEPT

The updates will be downloaded and installed. This may take several minutes.

The apps have been updated.
There are no other updates
available:

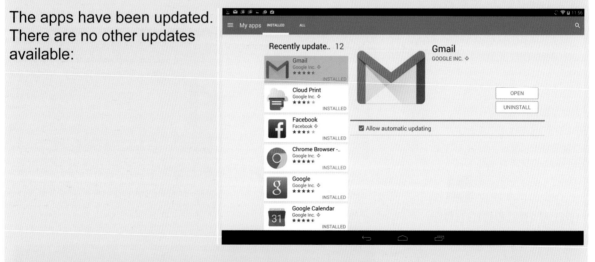

You can also disable the *Auto update* function entirely, for example if you are
worried about the costs of extra data charges. You can change the setting, so that
apps are updated only when a Wi-Fi Internet connection is available.

☞ **Tap**

☞ **Tap** ⚙ SETTINGS

- Continue on the next page -

☞ Tap
Auto-update apps
Auto-update apps at any

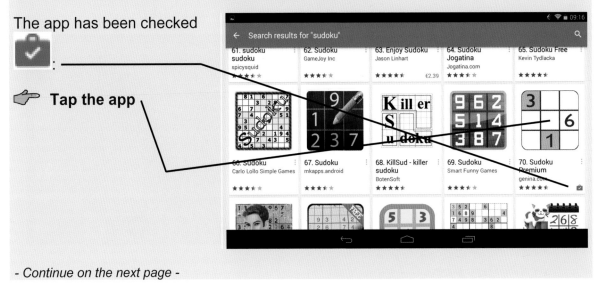

☞ **Tap the radio button**
⦿ **by**
Do not auto-update apps

Auto-update apps

Do not auto-update apps ○

Auto-update apps at any time. Data charges may apply. ⦿

Cancel

💡 **Tip**

Download a paid app once more
If you have uninstalled an app that you previously purchased, you can always download it again without an extra charge. You need to use the same *Google* account that was used to purchase the app originally:

The app has been checked

☞ **Tap the app**

- Continue on the next page -

The *Play Store* app will know that you have already purchased this app. Instead of the price you will see

INSTALL:

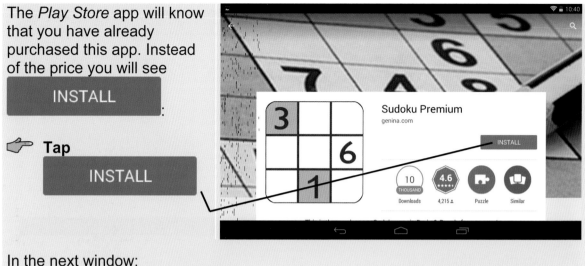

👉 **Tap**

INSTALL

In the next window:

👉 **Tap** **ACCEPT**

The app will be downloaded and installed. You will not be charged for the download.

💡 **Tip**

Adjust the favorites tray

The favorites tray can be found on the right-hand side or at the bottom of each page of the home screen. You can also replace the apps shown in the favorites tray with other apps. You do this in the same way as described earlier for moving apps on the home screen.

In this example you will be removing an app from the favorites tray:

👉 **Press and hold your finger on the desired app**

👉 **Drag the app to** ✕

👉 **Release your finger**

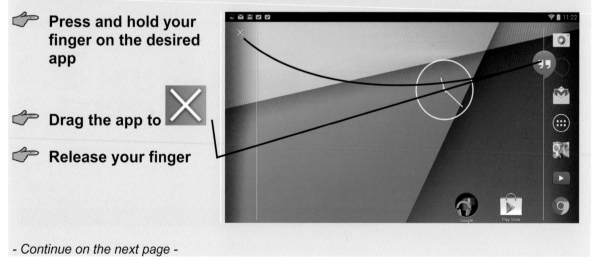

- Continue on the next page -

You can also move an app from the home screen to the favorites tray:

☞ **Press and hold your finger your finger on the app**

☞ **Drag the app to the favorites tray** ——

☞ **Release your finger**

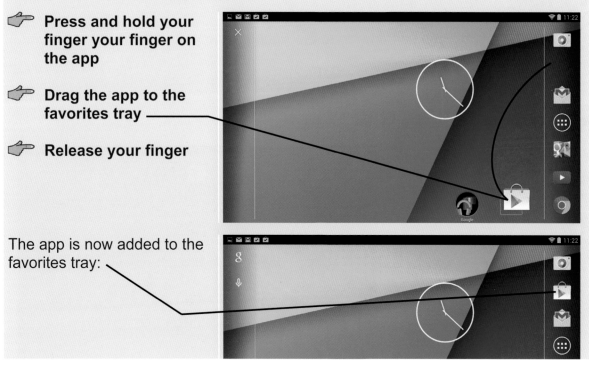

The app is now added to the favorites tray:

💡 **Tip**

Add an app to the home screen

You can also drag an app from the apps overview to the home screen:

☞ **Tap**

☞ **Press and hold your finger on the app**

☞ **Drag the app to the desired position on the home screen**

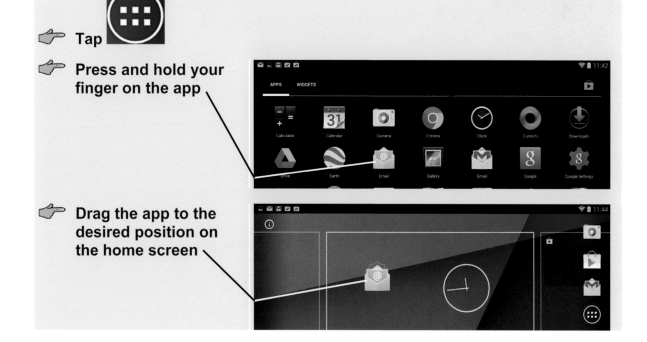

💡 Tip
Using the Facebook app
If you use *Facebook*, you can download the *Facebook* app and use it on your tablet:

☞ **Download the *Facebook* app** 👣¹⁷

☞ **Open the *Facebook* app** 👣⁸

You will need to sign in with your *Facebook* account, one-time only:

⌨ **Type your user name** ——

⌨ **Type your password** ——

👉 **Tap**

Log In

In the news feed you can see the posted messages from your friends and those from celebrities, organizations or the companies you follow. The messages you post on your own page, will appear in your friends' news feeds.

Tap 📝 **Status** to post a status message on your own *Facebook* page.
Tap 📷 **Photo** to select a photo or take a picture, and post it on your page with a caption or text.
Tap 📍 **Check In** to post a message regarding your current location on your page.

You will see the messages on your timeline. **About** let's you view the personal information you share on *Facebook*. **Photos** let's you view the photos you have uploaded to *Facebook*. **Friends** let's you view your list of friends.
Activity Log let's you view a summary of your recent activities on *Facebook*.

- Continue on the next page -

If somebody reacts to your message, or comments on a message to which you have commented, the ⊕ button will turn into ⊕2 . A red circle also appears by each new friend request by the 👥 icon and with a new private message by the 💬 icon.

You can use the search box 🔍 to find acquaintances or pages from companies, celebrities or organizations.

To view the other menu options:

☞ **Tap** ☰

Tap 📍 **Nearby Places** to see which friends are signed within the local area.

Tap 👤 **Find Friends** to look for friends and acquaintances in different ways.

Tap 👥 **Friends** to open your friends list.

Tap the 🖼 **Photos** app to view and manage your photos in *Facebook*.

At the bottom you will find the buttons for the help function and for editing the settings. If you stay signed in, new data will be retrieved as soon as you open the *Facebook* app. If you prefer to sign out, you can do that like this:

☞ **Tap** ⏻ Log Out

☞ **Tap** Log Out

💡 Tip

Using the Twitter app

If you use *Twitter*, you can download the *Twitter* app and use it on your tablet:

👉 **Download the *Twitter* app** 🐾¹⁷

👉 **Open the *Twitter* app** 🐾⁸

You will need to sign in with your *Twitter* account one-time only. On the bottom-right hand of the screen:

☞ **Tap**   Log in

☞ **Type your user name**

☞ **Type your password**

☞ **Tap**   Log in

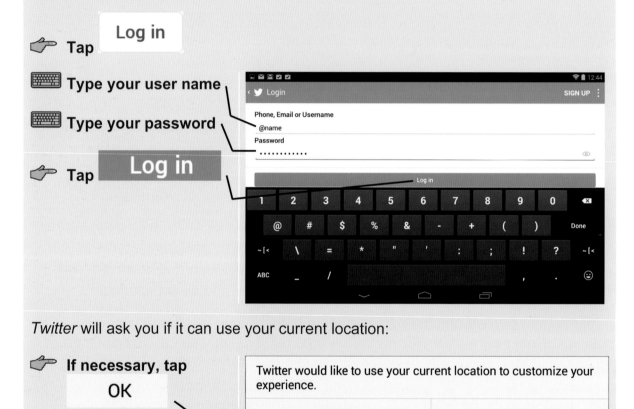

Twitter will ask you if it can use your current location:

☞ **If necessary, tap**

   OK

> Twitter would like to use your current location to customize your experience.
>
> Don't allow   OK

- Continue on the next page -

You will see your timeline, with the most recent tweets by the people or companies you follow. Your own tweets will appear in your followers' timelines.

This is how you load new tweets:

☞ **Swipe downwards over the screen**

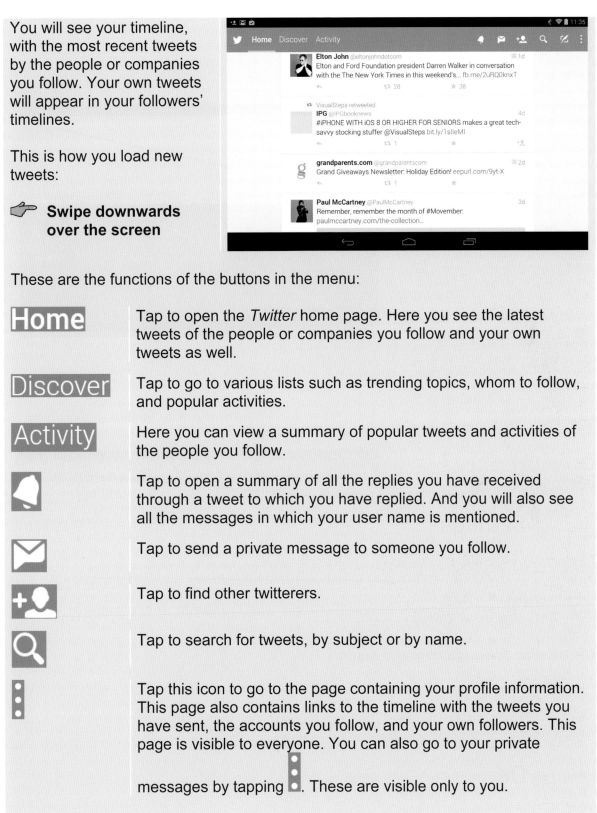

These are the functions of the buttons in the menu:

Home   Tap to open the *Twitter* home page. Here you see the latest tweets of the people or companies you follow and your own tweets as well.

Discover   Tap to go to various lists such as trending topics, whom to follow, and popular activities.

Activity   Here you can view a summary of popular tweets and activities of the people you follow.

🔔   Tap to open a summary of all the replies you have received through a tweet to which you have replied. And you will also see all the messages in which your user name is mentioned.

✉   Tap to send a private message to someone you follow.

👤+   Tap to find other twitterers.

🔍   Tap to search for tweets, by subject or by name.

⋮   Tap this icon to go to the page containing your profile information. This page also contains links to the timeline with the tweets you have sent, the accounts you follow, and your own followers. This page is visible to everyone. You can also go to your private messages by tapping ⋮. These are visible only to you.

- Continue on the next page -

To send a new tweet:

☞ **In the upper-right corner of the screen, tap**

⌨ **Type your message**

☞ **Tap**

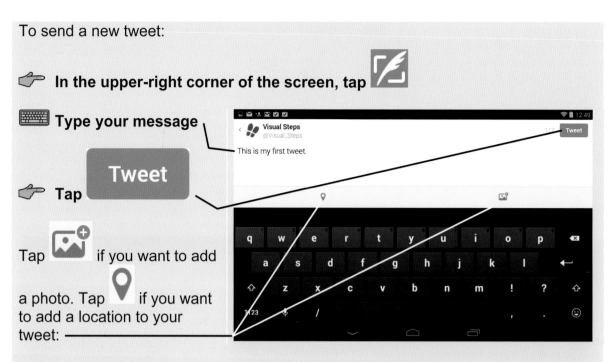

Tap [image] if you want to add

a photo. Tap [image] if you want to add a location to your tweet: ————

Your tweet will appear at the top of your timeline. Your followers will see your tweet appear in their timeline.

If you want to sign out, you can do that like this:

☞ **Tap**

☞ **Tap Settings**

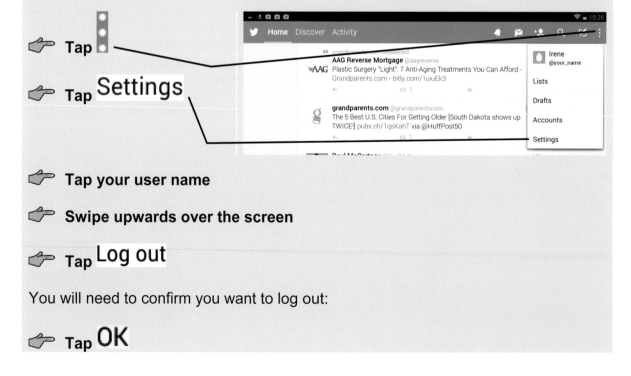

☞ **Tap your user name**

☞ **Swipe upwards over the screen**

☞ **Tap Log out**

You will need to confirm you want to log out:

☞ **Tap OK**

6. Photos and Video

Some tablets only have a camera on the front, whereas others have cameras on both the front and back side of the tablet. The camera on the front is mainly intended for taking self-portraits, and for video-chatting. If your tablet is also equipped with a camera on the back, you can use your tablet for taking pictures and recording videos.

You can copy photos and videos from your computer to your tablet and the other way around, from your tablet to your computer.

Your tablet contains one or more apps with which you can view photos and videos. In this chapter we discuss the standard *Camera* and *Gallery* apps. You can view photos on your tablet one at a time or as a slideshow. You can also edit photos with the *Gallery* app. You can use the *Email* app to send your photos by email.

In this chapter you will learn how to:

- take pictures and record videos with your tablet;
- copy photos and videos to your tablet;
- view photos;
- zoom in and zoom out;
- edit a photo;
- send a photo by email;
- play a video.

Please note:

If your tablet only has a camera on the front, you can skip *section 6.1 Taking Photos and Recording Videos*, or just read through it. In the *Tip Taking pictures with the front camera* on page 210 we explain how to take a self-portrait (selfie) with this camera.

Please note:

The screens you see on your own tablet may look different from the images in this book. The buttons may also have a different name or look a little different. Always search for a similar button or function. The basic operations will remain the same.

6.1 Taking Photos and Recording Videos

If your tablet is equipped with a camera on the back, you can take pictures and record videos with it. You can do this with the *Camera* app on your tablet.

☞ **Unlock or turn on the tablet** 👣¹

☞ **If necessary, tap**

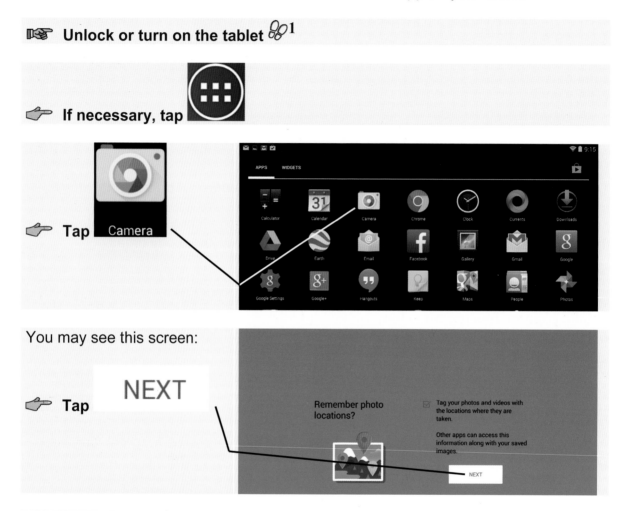

☞ **Tap** Camera

You may see this screen:

☞ **Tap** NEXT

Remember photo locations?

☑ Tag your photos and videos with the locations where they are taken.

Other apps can access this information along with your saved images.

NEXT

☞ **Point the camera toward the object you want to photograph**

💡 **Tip**

Sharpness

You can sharpen a part of a photo by tapping a specific area of the screen. On the place where you tap, a circle will appear [ ]. This will reorient the focus so that this part of the photo becomes sharper.

⤷ Please note:

Make sure to have sufficient light. Most tablets do not have a flash. If you take a picture while there is not enough light, the photo may look grainy.

This is how you take a picture:

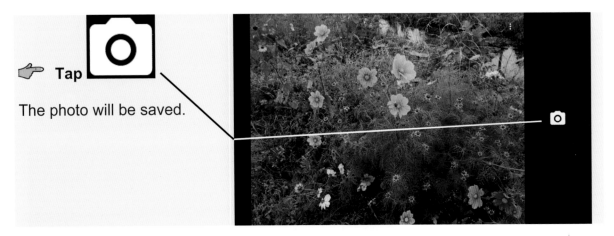

☞ Tap

The photo will be saved.

⤷ Please note:

The standard camera app on your tablet may differ from the app we have used in this chapter. The buttons may look a little different, and/or may be placed in a different spot on your screen. Your camera app may also have other options and functions.

♡ Tip

Switch to the camera on the front
You can also choose to use the camera on the front of the tablet. For example, to take a self-portrait (also called a *selfie*). To switch to the front camera:

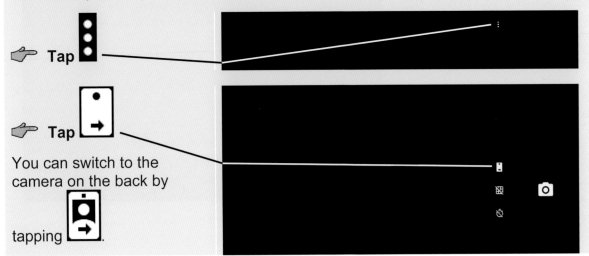

☞ Tap

☞ Tap

You can switch to the camera on the back by

tapping .

💡 Tip

Grid and self-timer

You can also choose to use a grid to make sure you take a straight photo and you can choose to use a self-timer:

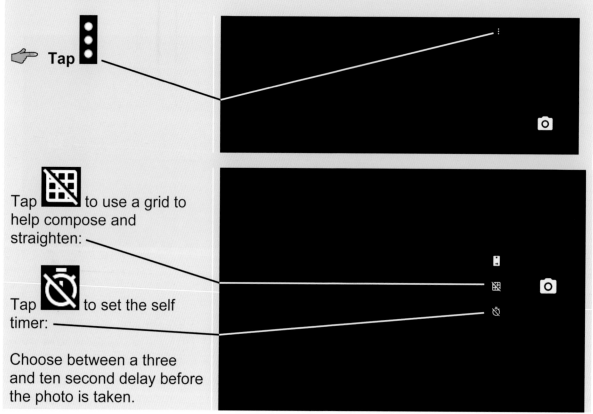

👉 **Tap** ⬛

Tap 🔲 to use a grid to help compose and straighten:

Tap 🚫 to set the self timer:

Choose between a three and ten second delay before the photo is taken.

You can also record video films with the *Camera* app. You do that like this:

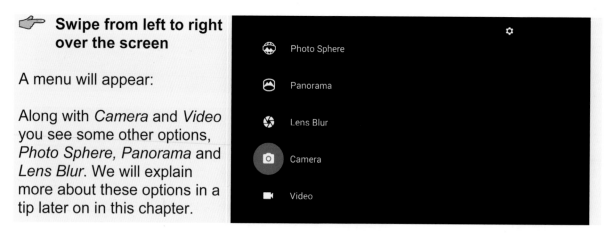

👉 **Swipe from left to right over the screen**

A menu will appear:

Along with *Camera* and *Video* you see some other options, *Photo Sphere, Panorama* and *Lens Blur*. We will explain more about these options in a tip later on in this chapter.

If you tap the gear icon you can change a few of the settings for the *Camera* app:

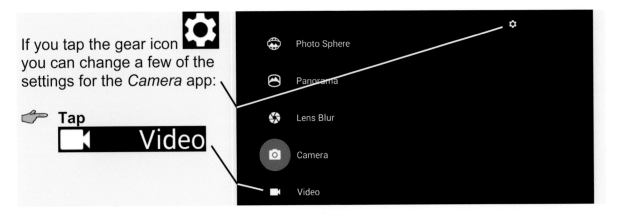

☞ **Tap**

☞ **Point the camera toward the object you want to film**

☞ **Tap**

The camera will start recording right away.

Stop the recording like this:

☞ **Tap**

The camera will stop recording, and the video will be saved.

☞ **Go to the home screen** ⅋⅋²

🩹 **HELP! I do not see the buttons at the bottom of the screen.**

Sometimes these buttons will disappear while using the *Camera* app. Tap the black bar shown at the bottom of your screen. The buttons 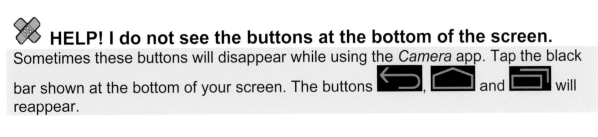 will reappear.

6.2 Copying Photos and Videos to Your Tablet

You can use *File Explorer* to copy photo and video files from your computer to your tablet.

☞ **Connect your tablet to the computer**

☞ **If necessary, close the *AutoPlay* window** ⚙²¹¹

☞ **Open *File Explorer* on your computer**

You can perform the following actions with a few of your own photos. You will be selecting multiple photos and copying them to your tablet:

☞ **Open the folder that contains the photos**

In this example we are using photos from the 🖼 **Pictures** folder.

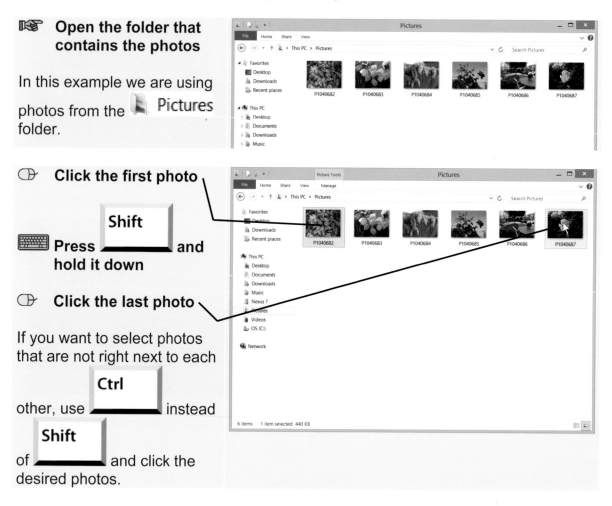

☞ **Click the first photo**

⌨ **Press** [**Shift**] **and hold it down**

☞ **Click the last photo**

If you want to select photos that are not right next to each other, use [**Ctrl**] instead of [**Shift**] and click the desired photos.

Right-click a photo

Click Copy

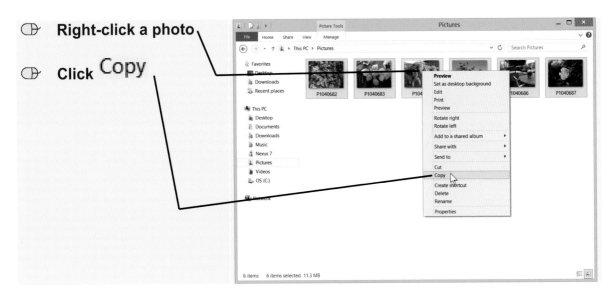

Your tablet will be recognized as a portable media device by *Windows*:

Click your tablet

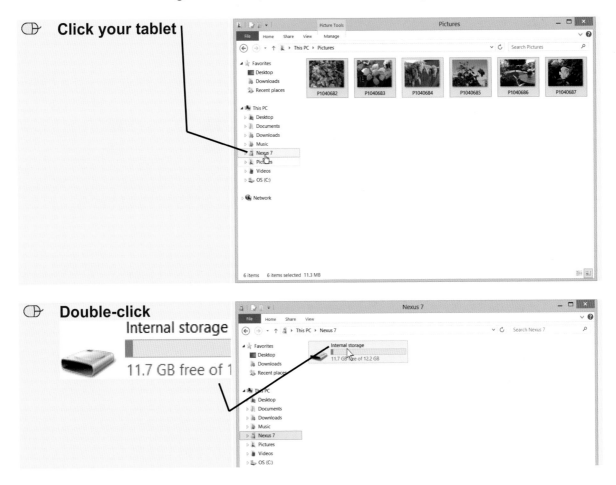

Double-click

Internal storage

11.7 GB free of 1

Double-click

Pictures

Right-click an empty section of the window

Click Paste

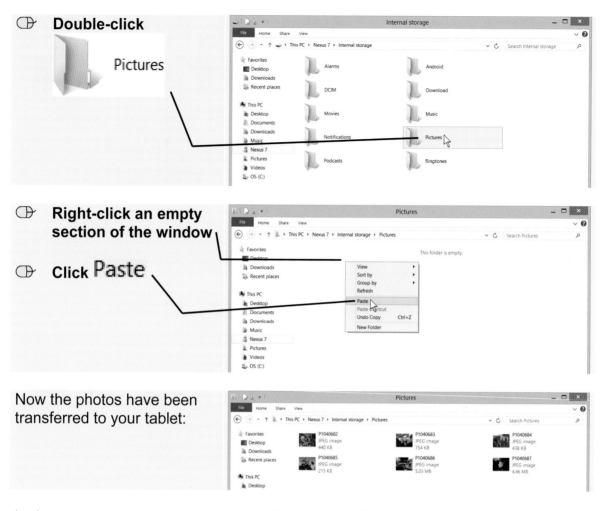

Now the photos have been transferred to your tablet:

In the same manner, you can copy a video to the *Movies* folder on your tablet:

☞ **Copy a video to the** **Movies** **folder on your tablet** ✇¹²

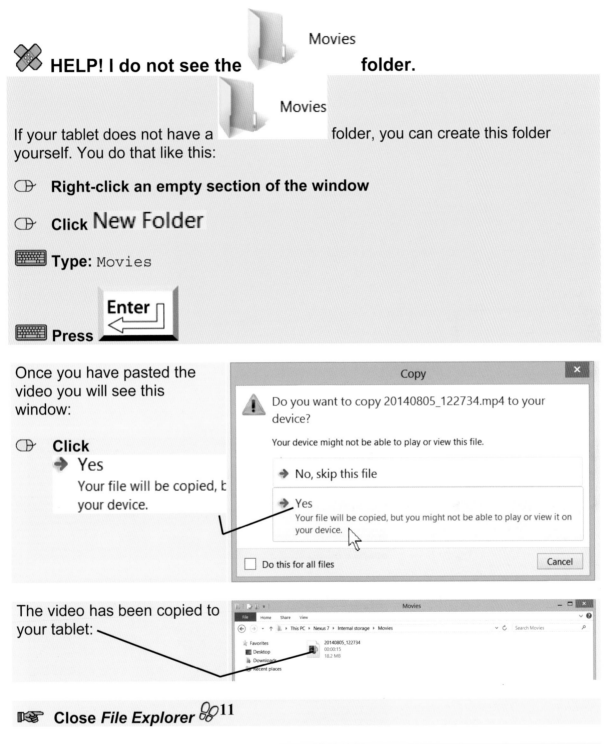

HELP! I do not see the Movies folder.

If your tablet does not have a Movies folder, you can create this folder yourself. You do that like this:

☞ **Right-click an empty section of the window**

☞ **Click New Folder**

⌨ **Type:** Movies

⌨ **Press** Enter

Once you have pasted the video you will see this window:

☞ **Click**
→ Yes
Your file will be copied, but your device.

Copy

⚠ Do you want to copy 20140805_122734.mp4 to your device?

Your device might not be able to play or view this file.

→ No, skip this file

→ Yes
Your file will be copied, but you might not be able to play or view it on your device.

☐ Do this for all files   Cancel

The video has been copied to your tablet:

Movies — This PC › Nexus 7 › Internal storage › Movies

Favorites
Desktop
Downloads
Recent places

20140805_122734
00:00:15
18.2 MB

☞ **Close** *File Explorer* 👣11

☞ **Disconnect your tablet from the computer**

Now you have copied a number of photo files and a video file to your tablet. In the next few sections you will be working with these files.

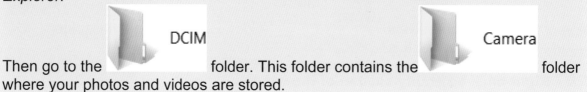

Tip

The other way round

You can also use the same method to copy photos and videos you have made with your tablet to your computer. In order to do this, you need to find your tablet in *File Explorer.*

Then go to the 

folder. This folder contains the 

folder where your photos and videos are stored.

6.3 Viewing Photos on Your Tablet

You can use the *Gallery* app to view the photos on your tablet. You can also use the *Photos* app or you can go to the *Play Store* app and find other apps with which you can view photos. In this section we will discuss the *Gallery* app.

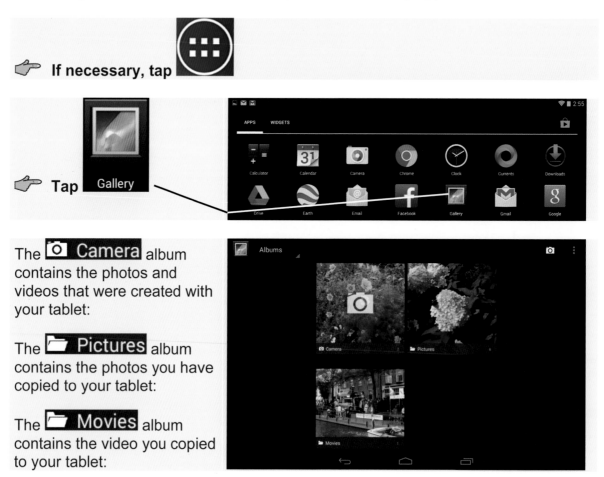

If necessary, tap 

Tap 

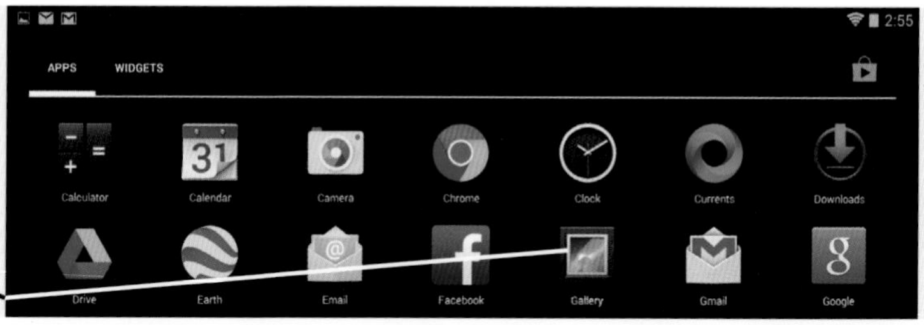

The Camera album contains the photos and videos that were created with your tablet:

The Pictures album contains the photos you have copied to your tablet:

The Movies album contains the video you copied to your tablet:

☞ **Tap the** 📁 **Pictures album**

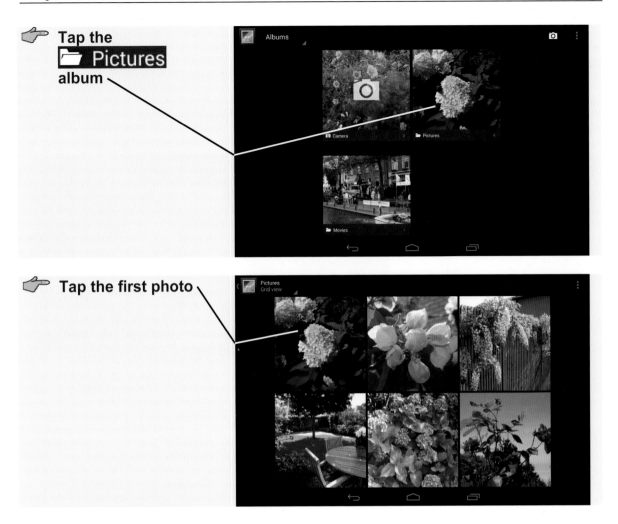

☞ **Tap the first photo**

The photo will be displayed full-screen. You can browse to the next photo like this:

☞ **Swipe from right to left over the screen**

You will see the next photo.

 Swipe once more from right to left

You will see the third photo. You can also zoom in on a photo. To do this, you need to use the touch gestures you previously learned, while surfing the Internet:

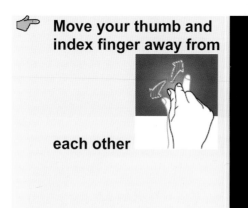 **Move your thumb and index finger away from**

each other

You will zoom in on the photo:

💡 **Tip**

Move

You can move the photo on which you have zoomed in by dragging your finger across the screen.

This is how you zoom out again:

👉 **Move your thumb and index finger towards each other over the screen (pinch)**

You will see the regular view of the photo again:

This is how you go back to the first photo:

👉 **Swipe from left to right over the screen, twice**

You can also view all the photos in an album as a slideshow. Like this:

Tap the photo

Tap

Tap Slideshow

The slideshow will start. To stop the slideshow:

Tap the screen once more

To go back to the list of all photos:

Tap

💡 **Tip**

Delete a photo

You can use *File Explorer* on your computer to delete photos on your tablet.
But you can also use the tablet itself to delete a photo. You can do that like this:

Tap the photo

Tap

Tap Delete

6.4 Editing a Photo

The *Gallery* app also has options for editing photos. To find these options:

👉 **Tap a photo**

👉 **Tap**

You will see various editing options:

* Tap [icon] to add an effect.

* Tap [icon] to add a decorative frame.

* Tap [icon] to crop, straighten, rotate, or mirror the image.

* Tap [icon] to enhance the color, lighting or contrast of the image.

You can practice using one of these options by trying out the cropping option:

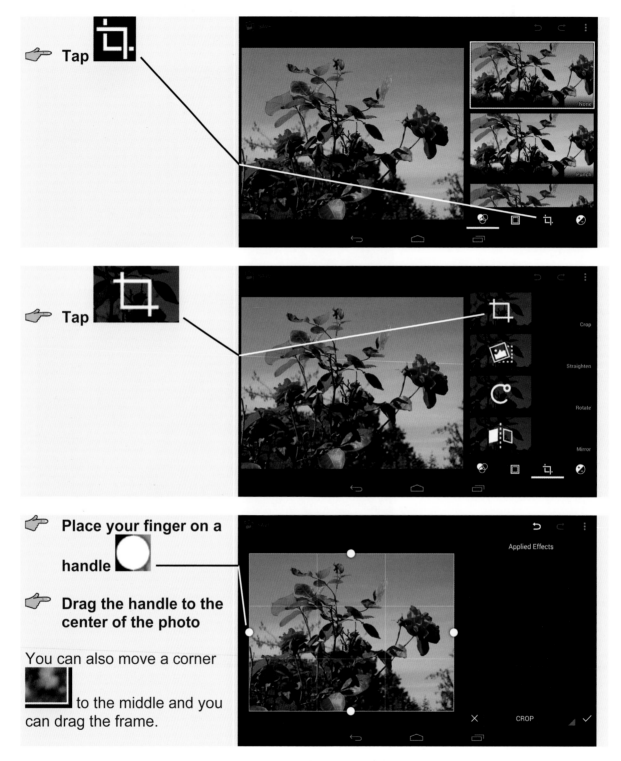

☞ **Tap**

☞ **Tap**

☞ **Place your finger on a handle**

☞ **Drag the handle to the center of the photo**

You can also move a corner

to the middle and you can drag the frame.

Tap **CROP** to select a different display format for the photo such as 4:3, 16:9 or square:

If you are satisfied with the result:

☞ **Tap** ✓

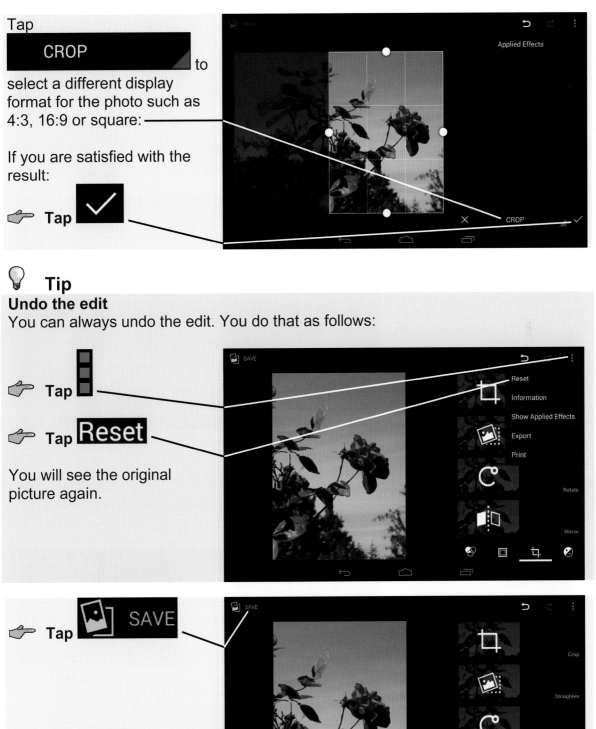

💡 **Tip**

Undo the edit
You can always undo the edit. You do that as follows:

☞ **Tap** ⣿

☞ **Tap** **Reset**

You will see the original picture again.

☞ **Tap** **SAVE**

You will see the edited photo:

To go back to the list of photos:

👉 **Tap**

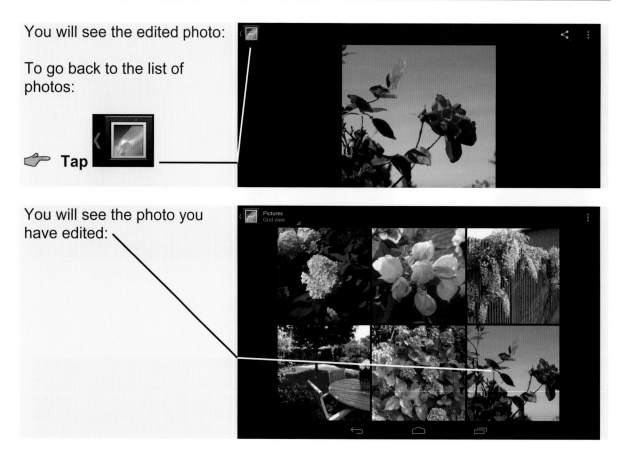

You will see the photo you have edited:

💡 **Tip**

Save the original photo
If you save the edited photo the original photo is overwritten. You can preserve the original photo by saving the edited photo as follows:

👉 **Tap** ⋮

👉 **Tap Export**

👉 **Tap Done**

The edited photo is saved separately and the original is preserved.

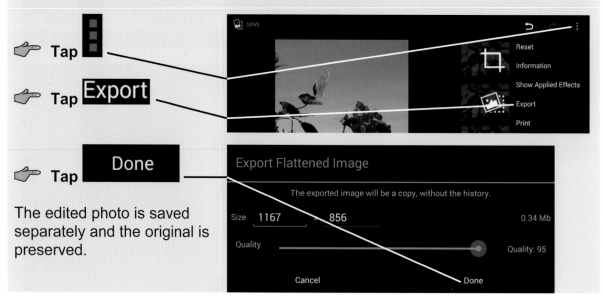

6.5 Sending a Photo by Email

If you have saved a nice photo on your tablet, you can share it in an email. You do that like this:

☞ **Open a photo** 👣¹³

👉 **If necessary, tap the photo**

👉 **Tap**

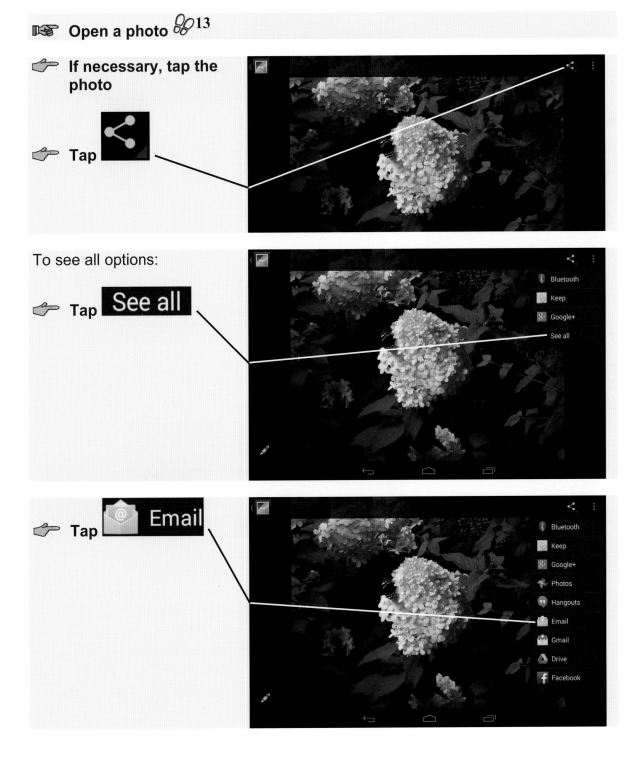

To see all options:

👉 **Tap** See all

👉 **Tap** Email

Now the photo has been added to the email, as an attachment: ——

You may need to drag up a little bit in order to see the photo.

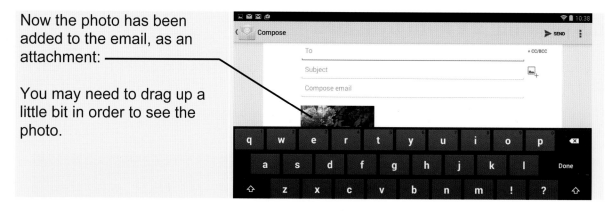

🖐 Please note:

If you have not yet added an email account to your tablet, you can read *section 2.1 Adding an Email Account to the Email App* to learn how to do so.

🩹 HELP! The file is too large.

If the file is too large to send it by email, you may want to look for an app in the *Play Store* app that can reduce the size of the photo. For example, *Resize me* and *Reduce photo*.

Now you can finish your email and send it, as explained in *section 2.2 Writing and Sending an Email Message*. For now this will not be necessary.

👉 **Tap** ⋮ ——

👉 **Tap Discard** ——

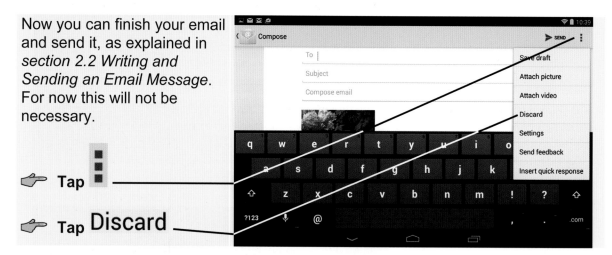

You will be asked whether you really want to delete the message:

👉 **Tap Discard** ——

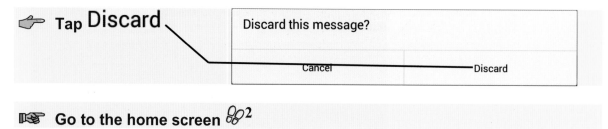

🖐 **Go to the home screen** 👣²

6.6 Playing a Video

You can use the *Photos* app to view the videos on your tablet.

☞ **Open the *Gallery* app** 🦶⁸

☞ **If necessary tap** [image] **until you see the album screen**

☞ **Tap the album with the video** ↘

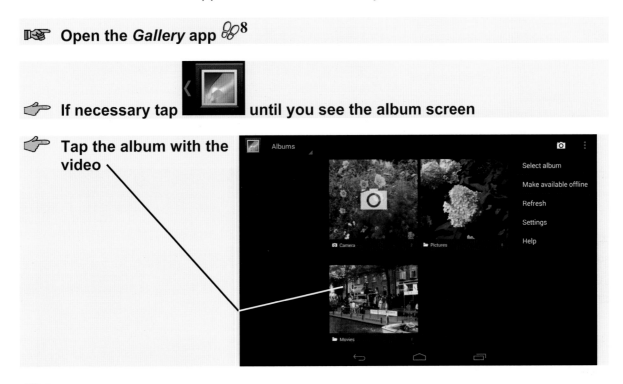

🐦 Please note:

If the video does not appear right away on your screen, it may be because the file format is not supported. You can try to download an app that does support the specific file format of this video file, such as *HD Video Player*. Your tablet may also already have another app with which you can view videos, such as *VideoPlayer*.

☞ **Tap** [▶]

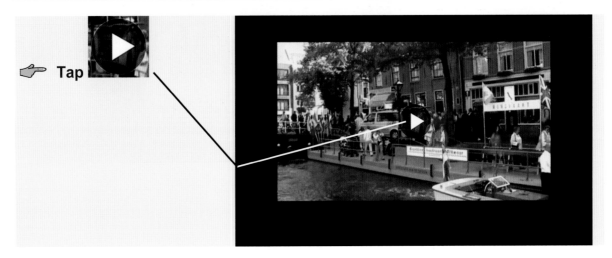

You can use the *Photos* app to view your videos, but you can also view them in the *Gallery* app.

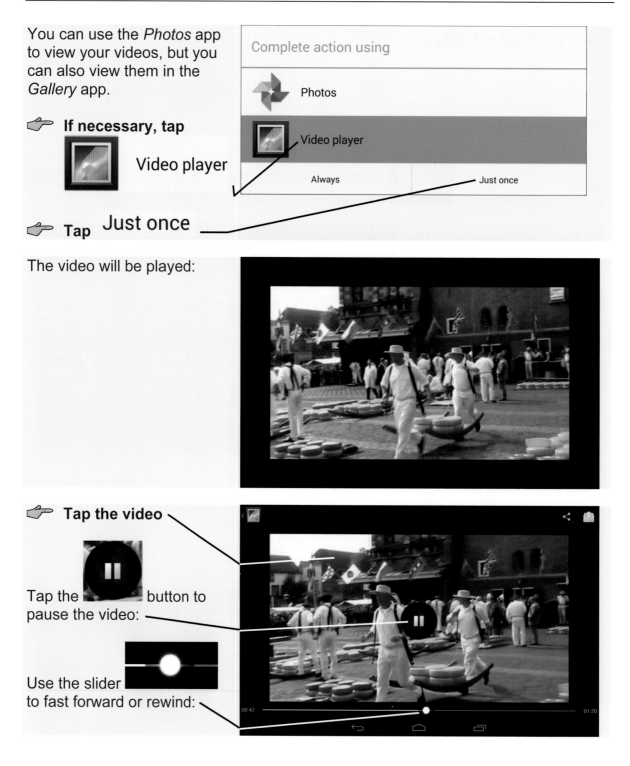

Complete action using

Photos

Video player

Always   Just once

☞ **If necessary, tap**

Video player

☞ **Tap** Just once

The video will be played:

☞ **Tap the video**

Tap the ❙❙ button to pause the video:

Use the slider to fast forward or rewind:

To go back to the list of all albums:

☞ **Tap** three **times**

☞ **Go to the home screen** ஓ²

💡 **Tip**

Delete a video

Deleting a video on your tablet is done in the same way as deleting a photo:

☞ **Tap the video**

☞ **Tap** ⋮

☞ **Tap** **Delete**

In this chapter you have learned how to take pictures and record videos with your tablet and how to view them. You have copied photos and a video from your computer to your tablet. You have also gotten acquainted with a few of the basic photo editing options and you have learned how to share photos in an email.

6.7 Background Information

Dictionary

Bluetooth	A wireless connection between two devices over a short distance. You can swap data between different devices through Bluetooth.
File Explorer	A *Windows* program with which you can organize and arrange your files.
Google Drive	A storage and synchronization service from *Google*. Your *Google* account can be used to upload and synchronize files to your *Google Drive* storage space on the Internet.
Google+	The social network offered by *Google*, comparable to *Facebook*.
Slideshow	A presentation or display of a series of pictures in sequence.
Zoom in	Take a closer look at an item. The letters and images become larger.
Zoom out	View an item from a distance. The letters and images become smaller.

Source: Wikipedia

6.8 Tips

Tip

Use the Photo Sphere effect

With the *Photo Sphere* option in the *Camera* app, you can create a three-dimensional picture of your environment. You can compare such a photo with *Street View* in *Google Maps*. It works like this:

☞ **Open the *Camera* app**
👣8

👉 **Swipe from the left side of the screen**

👉 **Tap**
🌐 Photo Sphere

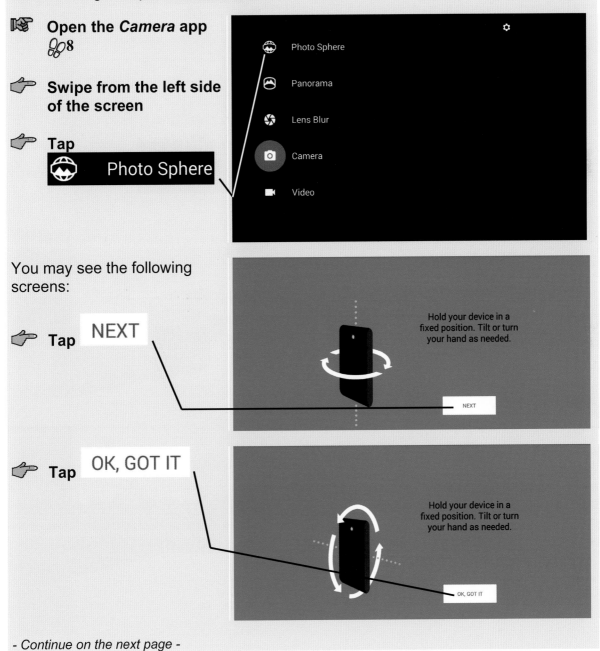

You may see the following screens:

👉 **Tap** NEXT

👉 **Tap** OK, GOT IT

- Continue on the next page -

☞ **Tilt to adjust the angle of your tablet so that the dot** 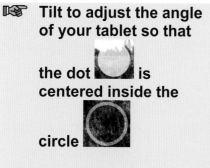 **is centered inside the circle**

A photo is taken automatically:

☞ **Rotate yourself slowly while holding the tablet. As the next dot appears, pause to align it with the center of the circle (also called the donut).**

The dot turns blue as soon as it is near the circle.

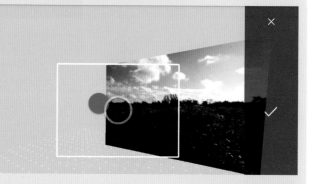

Each time the dot is centered inside the circle, a photo is taken:

☞ **Continue rotating towards the next dot**

In this way, you make a large number of photographs of the desired area.

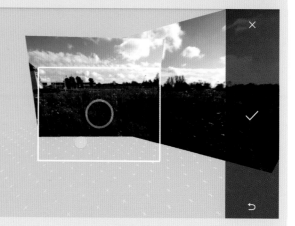

- Continue on the next page -

When you are satisfied:

☞ **Tap**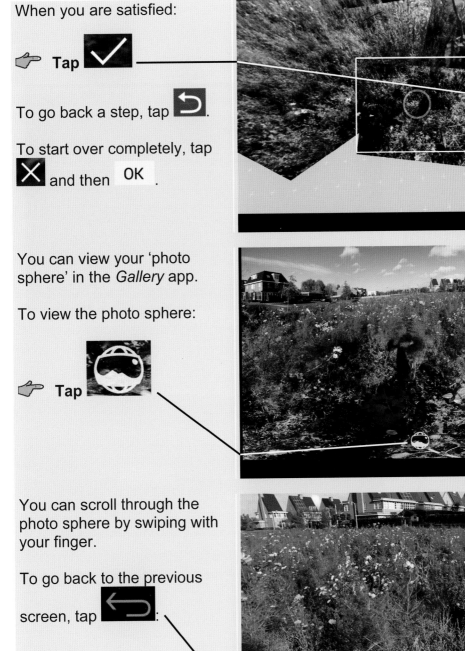

To go back a step, tap [icon].

To start over completely, tap [X] and then OK .

You can view your 'photo sphere' in the *Gallery* app.

To view the photo sphere:

☞ **Tap** [icon]

You can scroll through the photo sphere by swiping with your finger.

To go back to the previous screen, tap [icon]:

Tip
Make a panorama photo
You can use the *Camera* app to make a panorama photo:

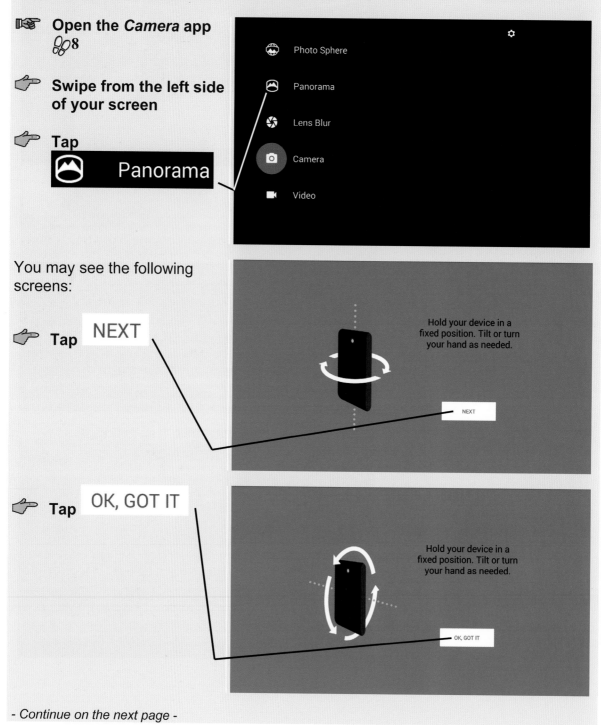

☞ **Open the *Camera* app**
👣8

👉 **Swipe from the left side of your screen**

👉 **Tap**

Panorama

You may see the following screens:

👉 **Tap** NEXT

👉 **Tap** OK, GOT IT

- Continue on the next page -

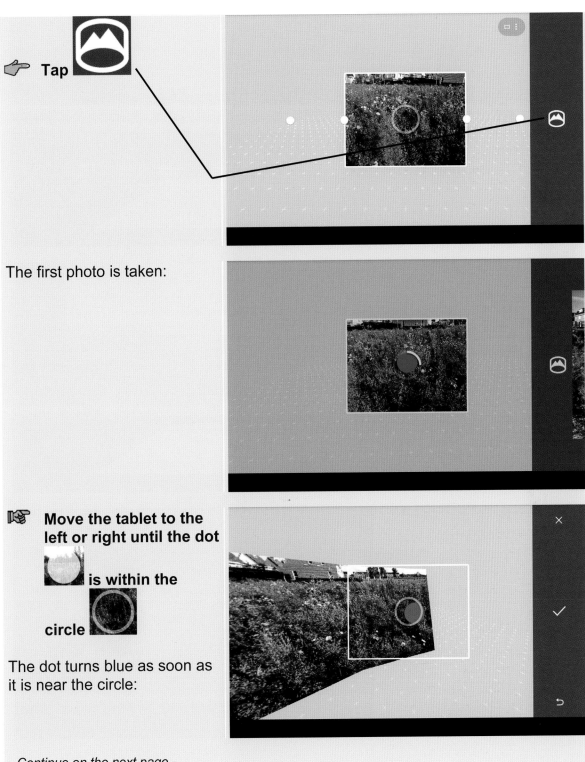

☞ **Tap**

The first photo is taken:

👉 **Move the tablet to the left or right until the dot is within the circle**

The dot turns blue as soon as it is near the circle:

- Continue on the next page -

Each time the dot is centered inside the circle, a photo is taken:

☞ **Rotate slowly until the next dot appears**

Continue rotating and taking pictures of the desired area.

When you are satisfied:

☞ Tap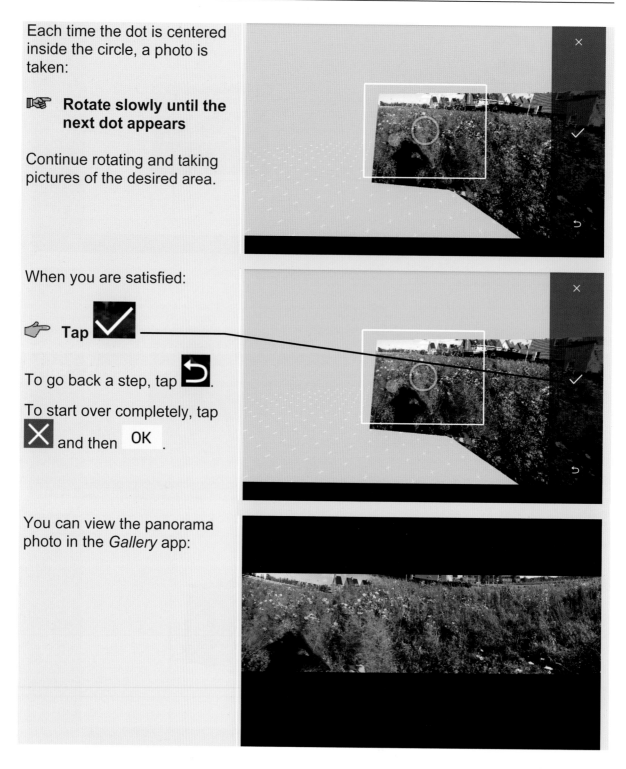

To go back a step, tap .

To start over completely, tap and then OK .

You can view the panorama photo in the *Gallery* app:

Tip

Use the Lens Blur effect

The *Lens Blur* will add a depth-of-field effect to a photo by bringing the subject in the photo in focus while blurring the background. This can make the subject in the foreground more pronounced. You use the *Lens Blur* option as follows:

Open the *Camera* app
♘8

Swipe from the left side of your screen

Tap
Lens Blur

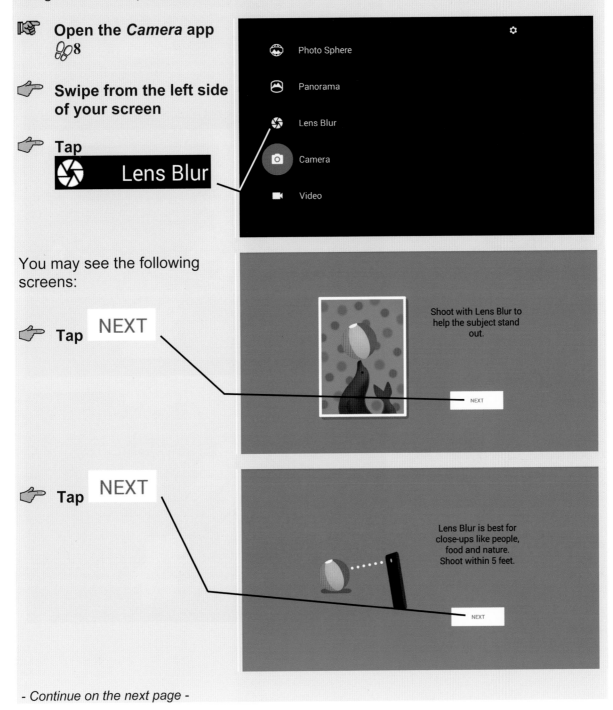

You may see the following screens:

Tap NEXT

Shoot with Lens Blur to help the subject stand out.

NEXT

Tap NEXT

Lens Blur is best for close-ups like people, food and nature. Shoot within 5 feet.

NEXT

- *Continue on the next page -*

☞ **Tap** OK, GOT IT

☞ **Point the camera towards the subject**

☞ **Tap**

☞ **Move the tablet slowly upwards**

If something has gone wrong, a warning will appear such as Device moved too fast.

You can start over by tapping

- Continue on the next page -

When you see a checkmark

, it means the photo has been taken:

You can view the photo in the *Gallery* app:

💡 Tip

Use a photo as a background (wallpaper) for the home screen

You can also use your own photo as a background for the home screen. You do that as follows:

☞ **Open the *Camera* app** 🐾8

☞ **Open a photo** 🐾13

👉 **If necessary, tap the photo**

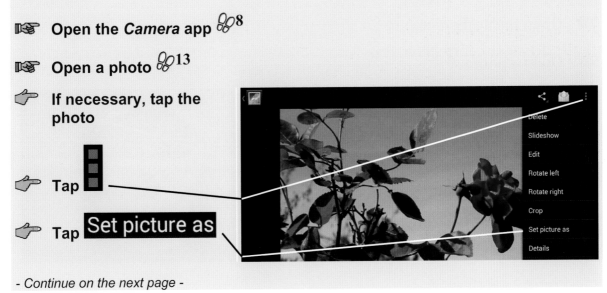

Delete
Slideshow
Edit
Rotate left
Rotate right
Crop
Set picture as
Details

👉 **Tap** ⬛

👉 **Tap** **Set picture as**

- Continue on the next page -

☞ **Tap**

| | **Set as** |
| ☐ | **Wallpaper** Gallery |

You can choose which part of the photo you want to use:

☞ **If desired, zoom in and drag the photo**

☞ **Tap**

✓ **SET WALLPAPER**

You can also change the background by using the *Settings* app and tapping the *Display* option. You can always revert back to a standard background if desired.

💡 **Tip**

Add a photo to a contact
In the same way, you can link a photo to one of your contacts:

👣 **Open the *Camera* app** 👣8

👣 **Open a photo** 👣13

☞ **If necessary, tap the photo**

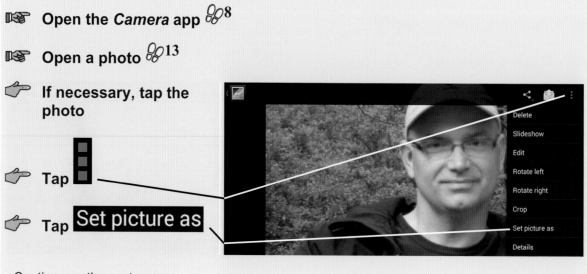

☞ **Tap** ⋮

☞ **Tap** Set picture as

- Continue on the next page -

👉 **Tap**
Contact photo

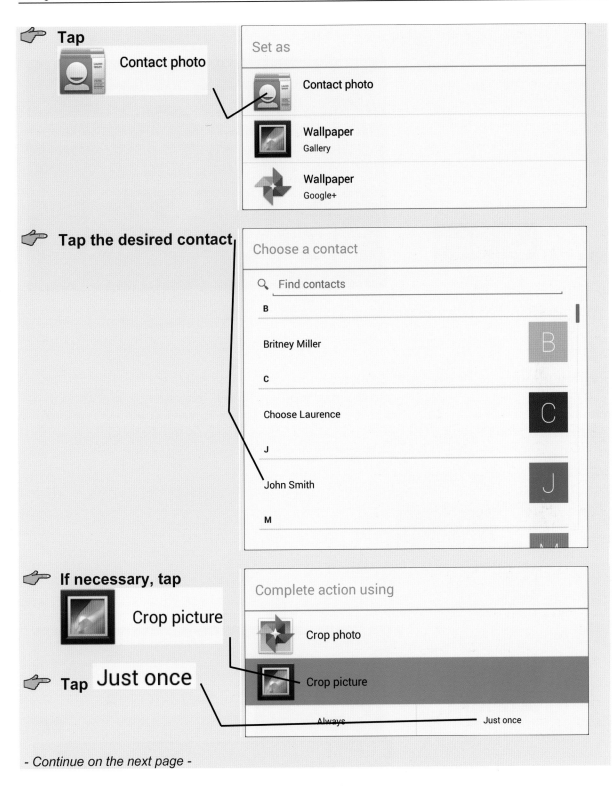

Set as

Contact photo

Wallpaper
Gallery

Wallpaper
Google+

👉 **Tap the desired contact**

Choose a contact

🔍 Find contacts

B

Britney Miller   B

C

Choose Laurence   C

J

John Smith   J

M

👉 **If necessary, tap**
Crop picture

👉 **Tap** Just once

Complete action using

Crop photo

Crop picture

Always   Just once

- Continue on the next page -

Select the part of the photo you want to use:

☞ **If desired, drag and move the handles**

☞ **If desired, drag and move the frame**

If you are satisfied with the photo:

☞ **Tap**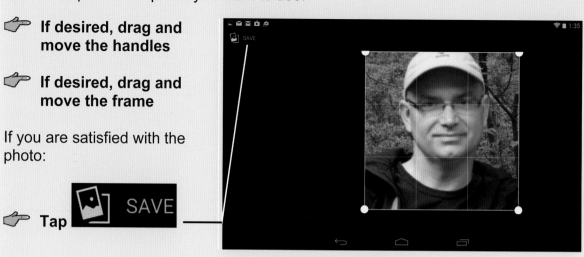

Now the photo has been added to this contact's information.

💡 **Tip**

Taking pictures with the front camera
A tablet that only has a front camera is really only suitable for taking self-portraits (selfies) or for video chatting. Some tablets may not even have a standard camera app installed. In that case you can download a camera app in the *Play Store* app:

☞ **Open the *Play Store* app** 👣8

☞ **Tap** APPS

☞ **Tap** 🔍

⌨ **Type:** camera

☞ **Tap**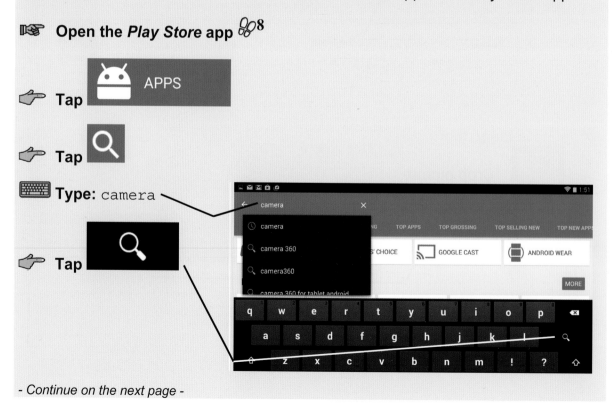

- Continue on the next page -

In this example, we will download and install the *Camera* app for *Android*:

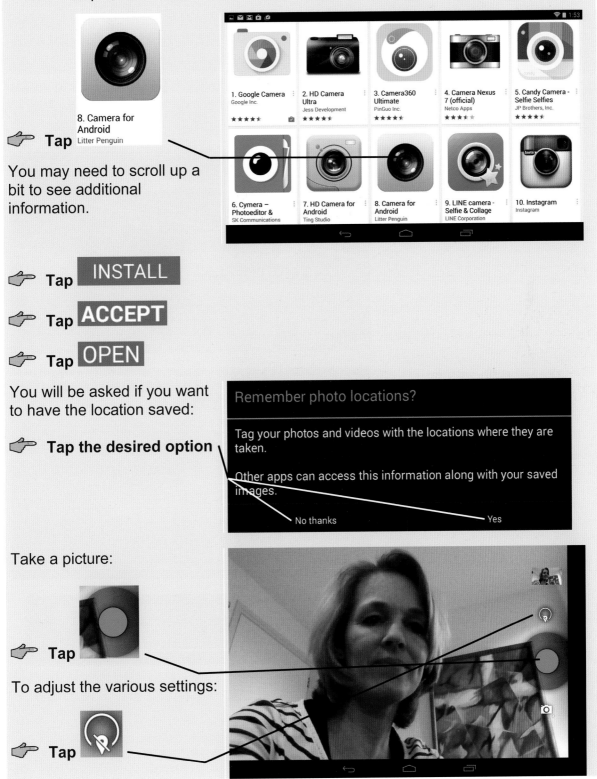

👉 **Tap** 8. Camera for Android Litter Penguin

You may need to scroll up a bit to see additional information.

👉 **Tap** INSTALL

👉 **Tap** ACCEPT

👉 **Tap** OPEN

You will be asked if you want to have the location saved:

Remember photo locations?

Tag your photos and videos with the locations where they are taken.

Other apps can access this information along with your saved images.

No thanks   Yes

👉 **Tap the desired option**

Take a picture:

👉 **Tap**

To adjust the various settings:

👉 **Tap**

Tip

Deleting multiple photos

In the *Gallery* app you can delete a photo or video one by one. But it is also just as easy to delete multiple photos at once:

☞ **Open the *Camera* app** 🐾8

☞ **Tap an album**

☞ **Tap** ⋮

☞ **Tap** Select item

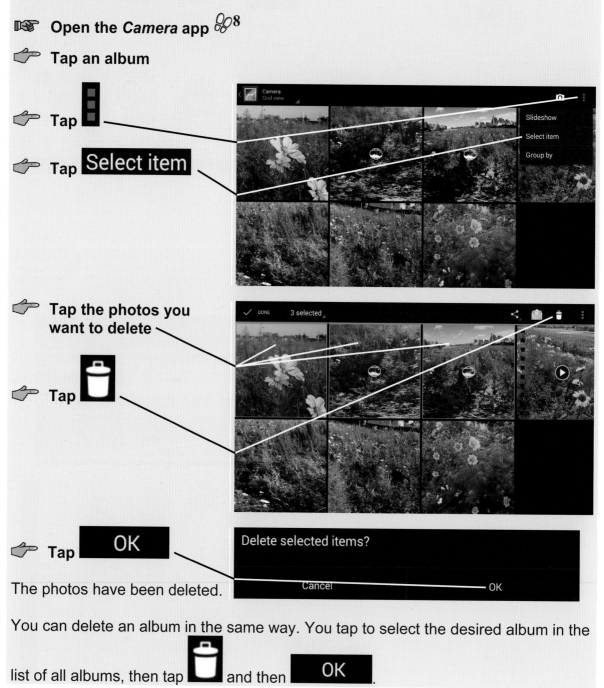

☞ **Tap the photos you want to delete**

☞ **Tap** 🗑

☞ **Tap** OK

The photos have been deleted.

You can delete an album in the same way. You tap to select the desired album in the list of all albums, then tap 🗑 and then OK .

7. Music

You can copy music from your computer to your tablet and then play it on your tablet. You can listen to your music with the *Play Music* app. This app also lets you easily create a playlist of your favorite songs.

You can purchase additional music in the *Play Store* app. You may also want to take a look at the *All Access* option. This service allows you to listen to millions of songs at a fixed monthly rate.

This chapter is mostly about copying music from your computer and then playing it on your tablet. The other options are briefly discussed at the end of the chapter.

In this chapter you will learn how to:

- copy music to your tablet;
- play music;
- create a playlist.

Please note:

In order to follow the examples in this chapter, you need to have some music files stored on your computer. If you do not have any music files or a computer for that matter, you can just read through this chapter.

Please note:

The screens you see on your own tablet may look different from the images in this book. The buttons may also have a different name or look a little different. Always search for a similar button or function. The basic operations will remain the same.

7.1 Copying Music to Your Tablet

You can copy the music files on your computer to your tablet with *File Explorer*.

☞ **Connect the tablet to the computer**

☞ **If necessary, close the *AutoPlay* window** 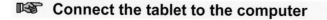¹¹

☞ **Open *File Explorer* on your computer**

You can perform the following operations with your own music. First you open the folder that contains the music files:

☞ **Open the folder that contains the music files**

In this example, the icons shown are located in the
🎵 Music folder:

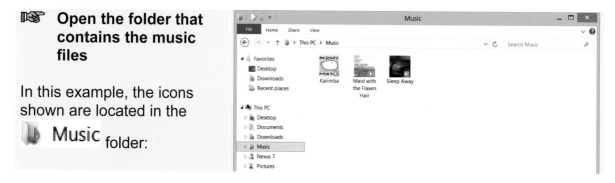

You start by selecting one or more files. Then you can copy them to your tablet:

👆 **Click the first file**

⌨ **Press** [**Shift**] **and hold it down**

👆 **Click the last file**

If you want to select files that are not adjacent to each other, use the [**Ctrl**] button instead of [**Shift**] and click the desired files.

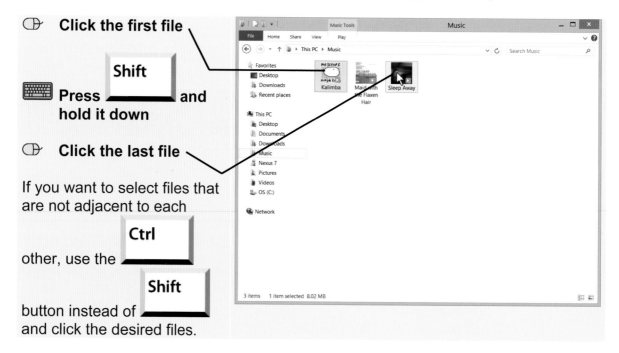

⊕ **Right-click a file**

⊕ **Click** Copy

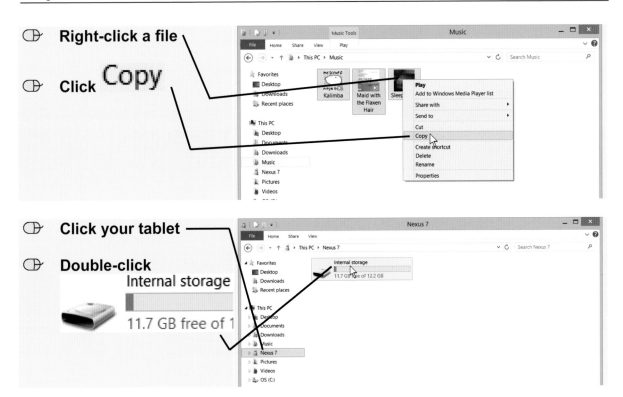

⊕ **Click your tablet**

⊕ **Double-click**
Internal storage

11.7 GB free of 1

In order to listen to the music with the *Play Music* app, the music files need to be copied to the *Music* folder. If you do not see this folder, it may not yet have been created. You can create this folder yourself. Here is how you do that:

⊕ **Right-click an empty section of the window**

⊕ **Click** New Folder

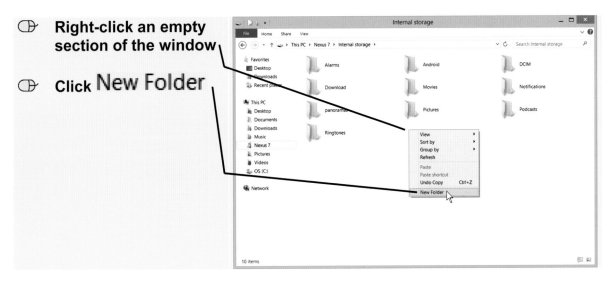

Type: `Music`

Click an empty section of the window

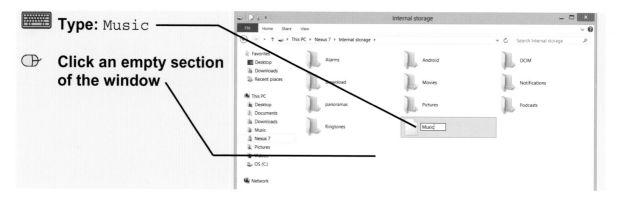

Now you can paste the music files in the *Music* folder:

Double-click

Music

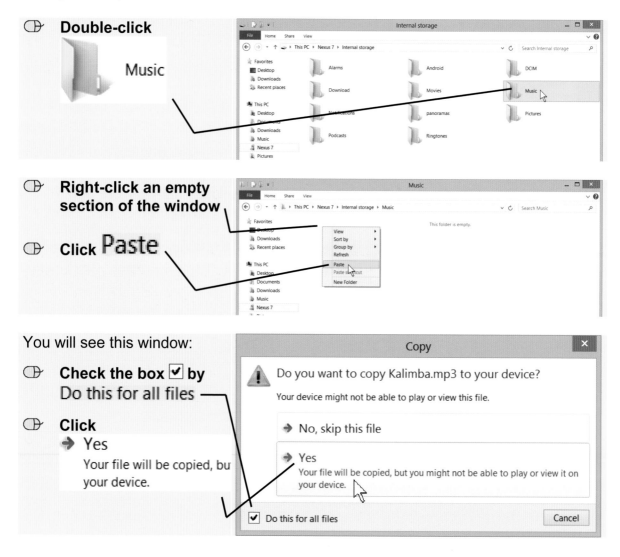

Right-click an empty section of the window

Click Paste

You will see this window:

Check the box ☑ **by** Do this for all files

Click
➜ Yes
Your file will be copied, bu your device.

The music files will be copied to your tablet. This may take a little while.

The music files have been copied to your tablet:

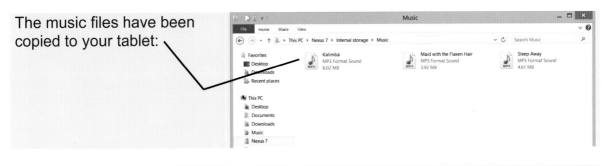

☞ **Close** *File Explorer* 👣11

☞ **Disconnect the tablet from the computer**

Now you have copied a number of music files to your tablet. In the next few sections you will begin to work with these files.

7.2 Playing Music

Your tablet is equipped with an extensive music player called the *Play Music* app.

➥ **Please note:**

Not all (music) file formats can be played in the *Play Music* app. If this is the case on your tablet, you can try to download an app that does support other file formats. We suggest for example, the *NRG Player* or the *Mobo music player*.

This is how you open the app:

👉 **Tap**

☞ **If necessary, swipe from right to left over the screen**

☞ **Tap** Play Music

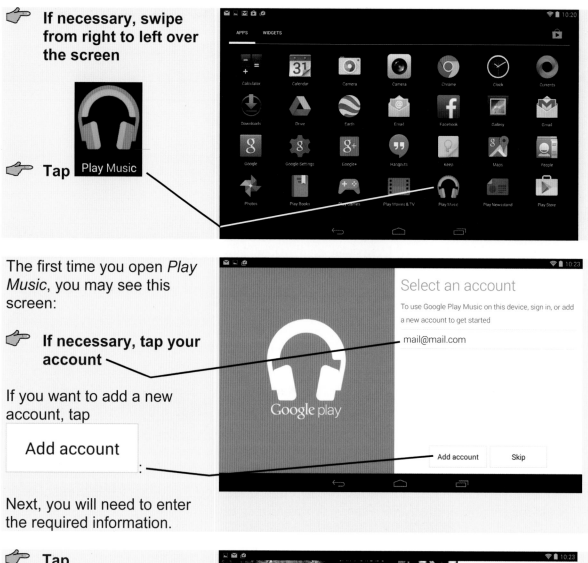

The first time you open *Play Music*, you may see this screen:

☞ **If necessary, tap your account**

If you want to add a new account, tap

Add account

Next, you will need to enter the required information.

☞ **Tap**

Use Standard

You can also tap **Get Started** to subscribe to *All Access*. This service lets you listen to millions of songs at a fixed monthly rate. It is very similar to *Spotify*. You can try *All Access* for free for 30 days.

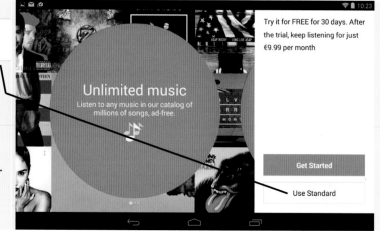

☞ **Tap Done**

In the **Listen Now** screen you will find music based on previously played tracks:

☞ **Tap** ☰

☞ **Tap** 🎵 **My Library**

You will see the artist view:

☞ **Tap an artist**

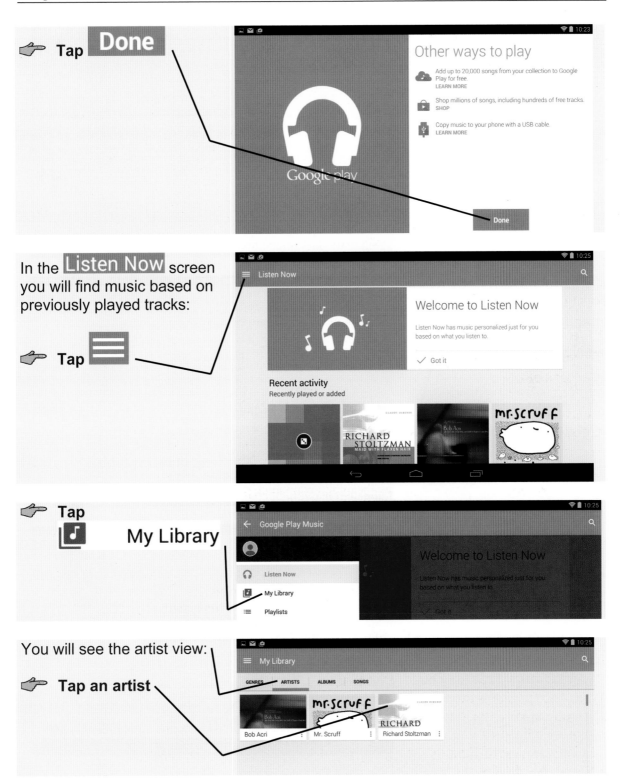

Tap the album's icon

If necessary, swipe upwards to see the first track

Tap the first track

You will see three buttons:

To see additional information:

Drag the bottom bar upwards

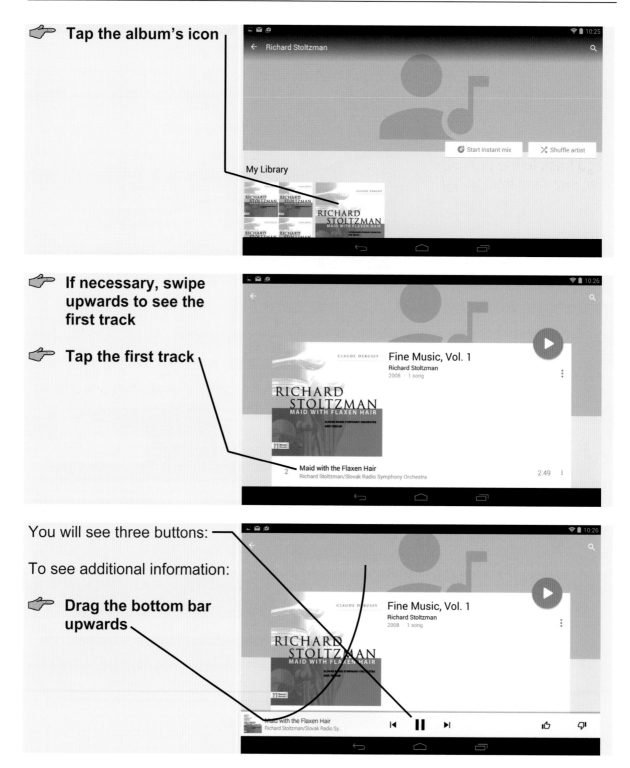

You will see the image on a full screen:

At the bottom of the screen you will find two more options:

To go back to the previous view, just drag the top bar downwards again.

The buttons on this bar have the following functions:

	Drag the slider or tap the line to find a specific section of the track.
	Tap this button to skip to the next track on the album. If the album contains only one song, the song will be played from the beginning.
	Tap this button to go back to the beginning of the song. Tap twice to go back to the previous track on the album.
	Tap to pause play.
	Tap to resume play.
	Tap to play in random order (shuffle). The button will turn orange .
	Repeat: • tap once: all the tracks on the album will be repeated. The button will turn orange . • tap twice: the current track will be repeated. The button will turn orange .

While the music is playing, you can quit the *Play Music* app and do something else:

☞ **Go to the home screen** 𝄞²

The music will continue to play. You can display the *Play Music* control buttons in any other app:

In the upper-left corner of the screen you will see the *Play*

Music icon 🎧 :

☞ **Place your finger on the icon and drag downwards**

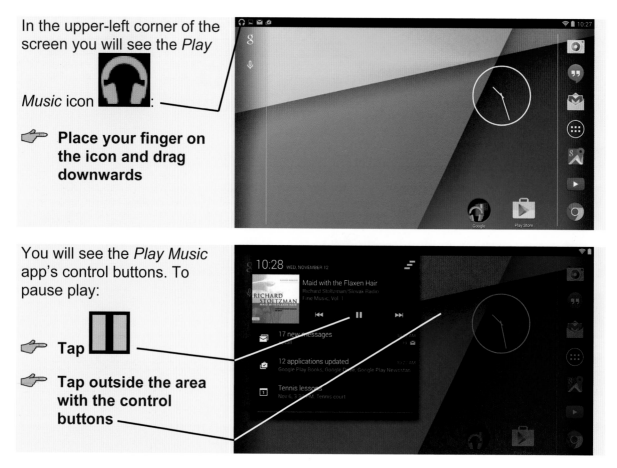

You will see the *Play Music* app's control buttons. To pause play:

☞ **Tap** ⏸

☞ **Tap outside the area with the control buttons**

You will see the tablet's home screen again.

7.3 Creating a Playlist

One of the nice things you can do with the *Play Music* app is to create a playlist. In a playlist, you can add your favorite songs and arrange them in any order you want. You can then play this list over and over again. Open the *Play Music* app again:

☞ **Open the *Play Music* app** 𝄞⁸

You will still see the screen with the last song you have played. Go back to the app's home screen:

In the upper-left corner of the screen:

☞ **Tap the track**

In this example, it is

Maid with the Flaxen Hair
Richard Stoltzman/Slovak Radio S

☞ **Tap** ⬅ **twice**

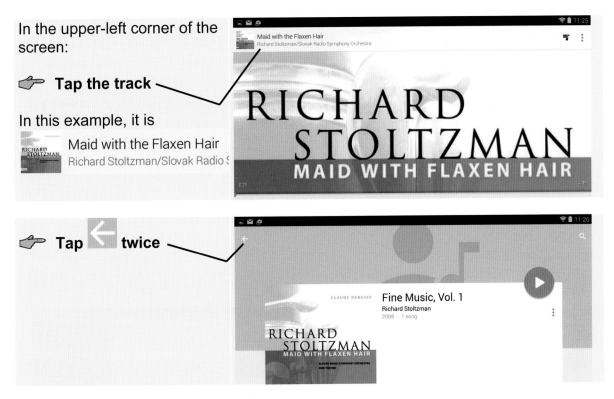

First, you open the *Songs* view

☞ **Tap SONGS**

☞ **By the desired song,**

tap ⦂

☞ **Tap** Add to playlist

☞ **Tap** New playlist

⌨ **Type a name, for example:** My favorite songs

☞ **If necessary, tap**

☞ **Tap** Create playlist

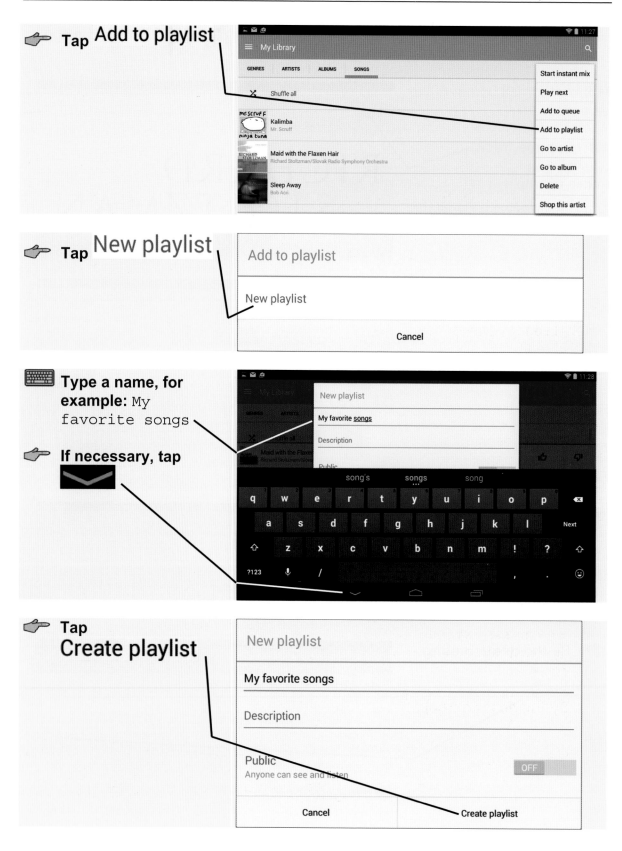

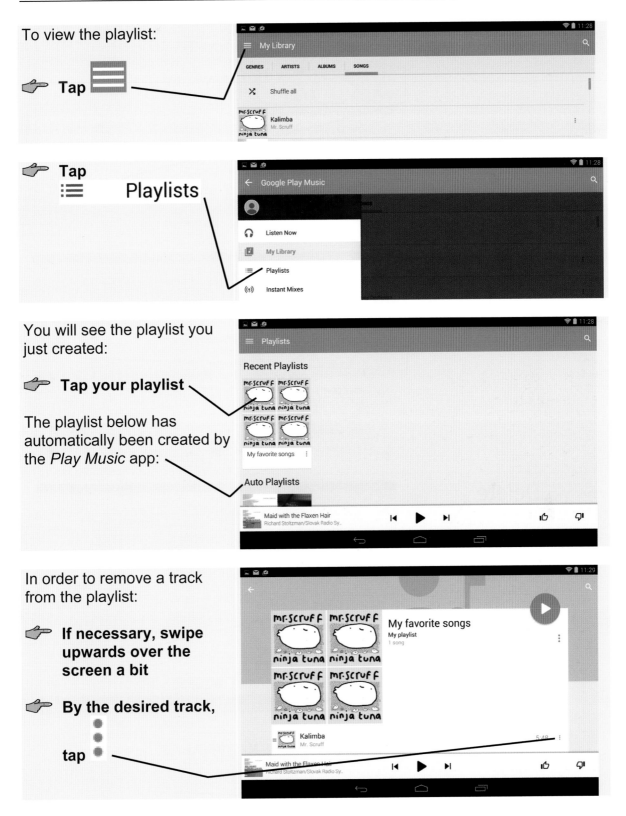

To view the playlist:

☞ **Tap** ☰

☞ **Tap**
☰ **Playlists**

You will see the playlist you just created:

☞ **Tap your playlist**

The playlist below has automatically been created by the *Play Music* app:

In order to remove a track from the playlist:

☞ **If necessary, swipe upwards over the screen a bit**

☞ **By the desired track,**

tap ⋮

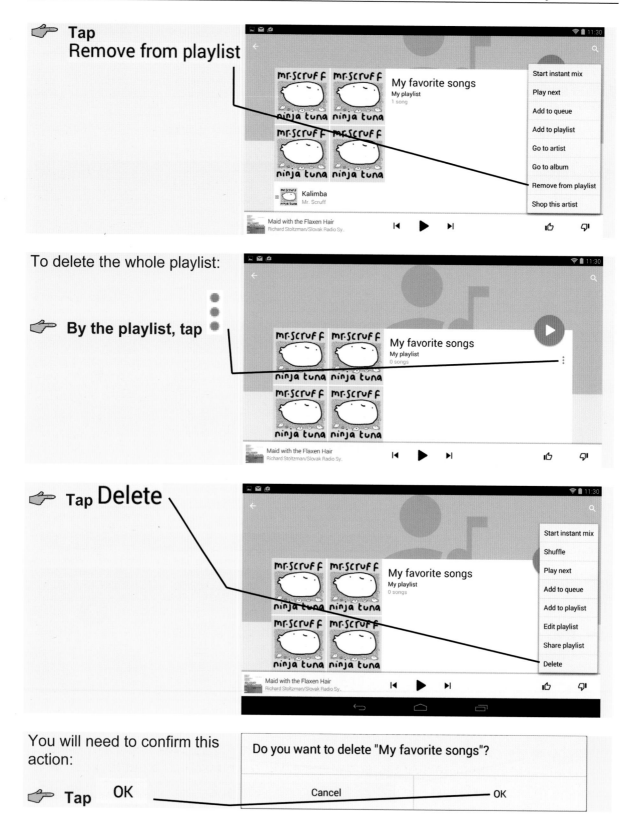

☞ **Tap**
Remove from playlist

To delete the whole playlist:

☞ **By the playlist, tap**

☞ **Tap Delete**

You will need to confirm this action:

☞ **Tap** **OK**

Do you want to delete "My favorite songs"?

Cancel   OK

💡 Tip

Deleting songs

You can use *File Explorer* on your computer to delete songs from your tablet. But you can also do this on your tablet using the *Play Music* app. To remove a song:

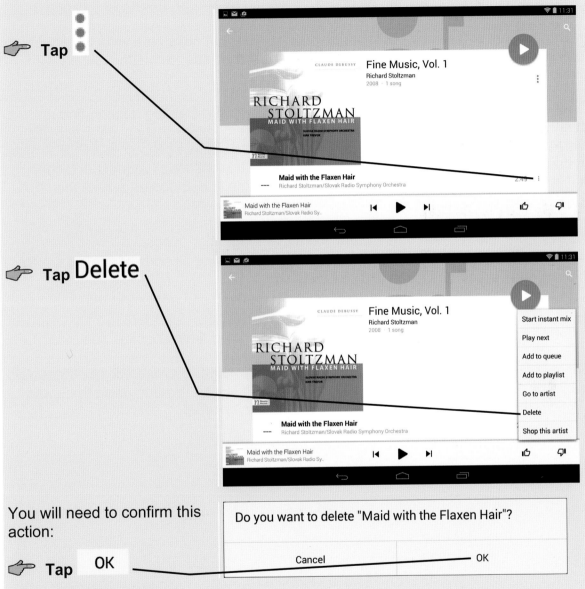

👉 **Tap** ⋮

👉 **Tap** Delete

You will need to confirm this action:

Do you want to delete "Maid with the Flaxen Hair"?

Cancel   OK

👉 **Tap** OK

The song will be deleted.

In this book you have learned how to work with your tablet by exploring many of its useful and handy functions. At the end of this chapter you will find a number of *Tips*. Now start enjoying your tablet.

7.4 Visual Steps Website and More Books

By now we hope you have noticed that the Visual Steps method is an excellent method for quickly and efficiently learning more about tablets, computers and other devices and their applications. All books published by Visual Steps use this same method.

In various series, we have published a large number of books on a wide variety of topics, including *Windows*, *Mac OS X,* the iPad, the iPhone*,* Samsung Galaxy Tab, photo editing and many other topics.

On the **www.visualsteps.com** website you can click the Catalog page to find an overview of all the Visual Steps titles, including an extensive description. Each title allows you to preview the full table of contents and a sample chapter in a PDF format. In this way, you can quickly determine if a specific title will meet your expectations. All titles can be ordered online and are also available in bookstores across the USA, Canada, United Kingdom, Australia and New Zealand.

Furthermore, the website offers many extras, among other things:
- free computer guides and booklets (PDF files) covering all sorts of subjects;
- frequently asked questions and their answers;
- information on the free Computer Certificate that you can acquire at the certificate's website **www.ccforseniors.com**;
- a free notify-me service: receive an email as soon as a new book is published.

There is far more to learn. Visual Steps offers lots of other books on computer-related subjects. And remember: each Visual Steps book has been written using the same step-by-step method with screenshots illustrating every step.

7.5 Background Information

Dictionary

All Access	This service lets you listen to millions of songs at a fixed monthly rate.
File Explorer	A *Windows* program for managing files and folders.
Play Music	An app with which you can listen to music on your tablet.
Play Store	An online store where you can download free and paid apps, games, films, music, and books.
Playlist	A collection of songs, arranged in a certain order.
Queue	The *Play Music* app organizes the tracks that are scheduled to be played in a *queue*. They are arranged in the order that you have given. You can add and remove tracks from this music queue.
Shuffle	Playing music tracks in random order.

Source: User manual Polaroid tablet, Wikipedia

7.6 Tips

💡 **Tip**

The Thumbs up playlist
You can make sure a certain song is played by adding it to the *Thumbs up* playlist:

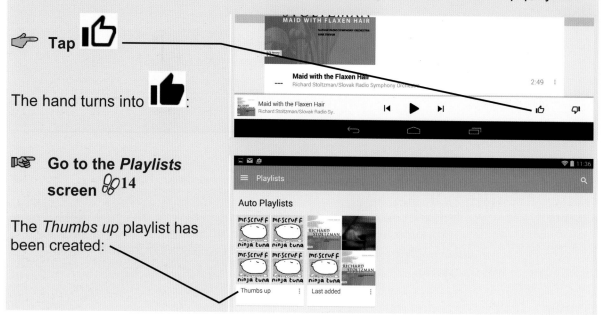

☞ **Tap** 👍 ————————

The hand turns into 👍:

☞ **Go to the *Playlists* screen** 𝄐14

The *Thumbs up* playlist has been created:

💡 **Tip**

The music queue
By placing tracks in a queue, they will be played in the order in which you place them. You can add a track to the queue as follows:

☞ **Select the *Songs* view** 𝄐15

☞ **By the desired song,**

⁞

tap ⁞ ————————

- Continue on the next page -

☞ **Tap** Add to queue

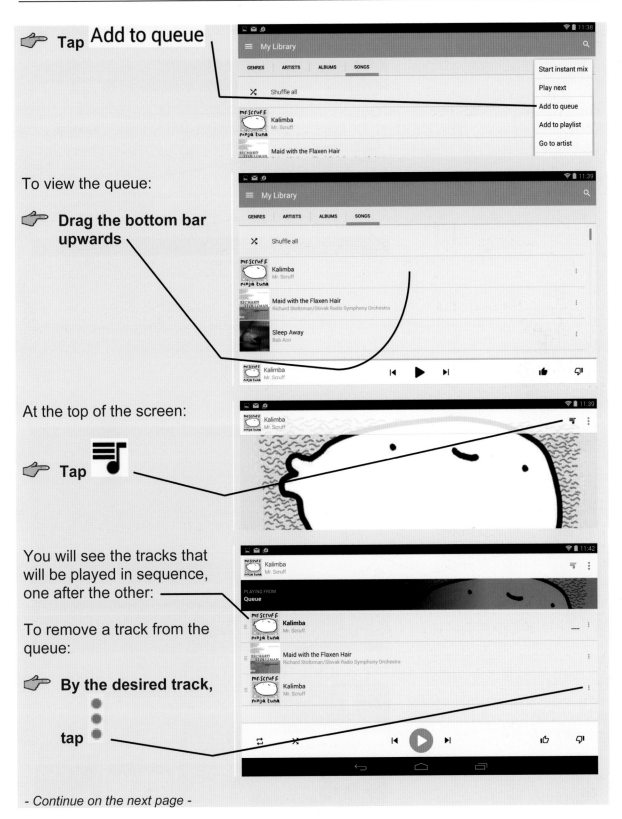

To view the queue:

☞ **Drag the bottom bar upwards**

At the top of the screen:

☞ **Tap**

You will see the tracks that will be played in sequence, one after the other:

To remove a track from the queue:

☞ **By the desired track,**

tap ⋮

- Continue on the next page -

👉 **Tap**
Remove from queue

💡 **Tip**
Buy music
You can also buy music in the *Play Store* app. You open the store from within the *Play Music* app:

👉 **Tap** ☰

👉 **Tap** 🛍 **Shop**

You can create an ((•)) **Instant Mixes** with the songs you have purchased:

You will see the *Music* screen of the *Play Store* app:

Music is purchased in the same way as you buy apps. See *section 5.2 Downloading a Paid App* for more information.

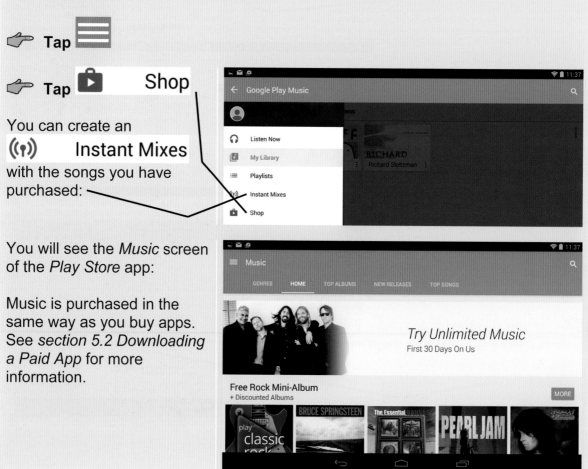

Appendix A. How Do I Do That Again?

The actions and exercises in this book are marked with footsteps: 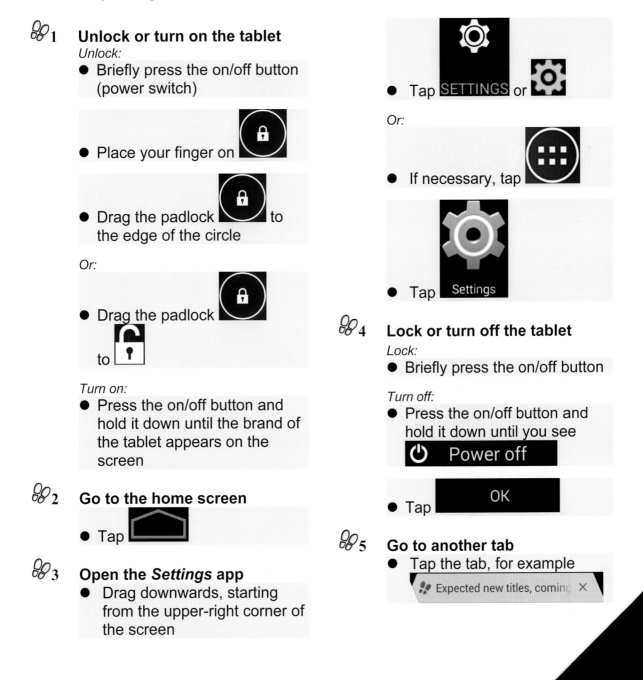1
If you have forgotten how to do something, you can read how to do it again by finding the corresponding number in the list below.

1 **Unlock or turn on the tablet**

Unlock:
- Briefly press the on/off button (power switch)

- Place your finger on

- Drag the padlock to the edge of the circle

Or:
- Drag the padlock to

Turn on:
- Press the on/off button and hold it down until the brand of the tablet appears on the screen

2 **Go to the home screen**
- Tap

3 **Open the *Settings* app**
- Drag downwards, starting from the upper-right corner of the screen

- Tap SETTINGS or

Or:
- If necessary, tap

- Tap Settings

4 **Lock or turn off the tablet**

Lock:
- Briefly press the on/off button

Turn off:
- Press the on/off button and hold it down until you see ⏻ Power off

- Tap OK

5 **Go to another tab**
- Tap the tab, for example Expected new titles, coming ✕

✇6   Add a contact

- Tap

- If necessary, tap **OK**

- Type the information for this contact

- Tap ✓ **DONE**

✇7   Disable location services

- Open the *Settings* app ✇3

- Tap 📍 **Location**

In general:

- Tap **ON**

For Google apps:

- Tap

  8 Google Location Reporting

- Tap **Location Reporting**

- Tap **ON**

✇8   Open an app

- Tap

- ~~Tap the app~~

~~app~~
~~our finger on the app~~

~~e app to the border of~~
~~een~~

When you see the other page:

- Release your finger

✇10   Delete an app

- Place your finger on the app

- Drag the app to ✕

- Release your finger

✇11   Close the window

- Click ✕

✇12   Copy file(s) from the computer to the tablet

- Connect your tablet to your computer

On your computer:

- If necessary, close the *AutoPlay* window ✇11

- Open *File Explorer*

- Open the desired folder

- Select one or more files

- Right-click a file

- Click **Copy**

- Click your tablet

- Double-click
  Internal storage
  11.7 GB free of 12.2 GB

- Open the desired folder

- Right-click an empty section of the window

- Click **Paste**

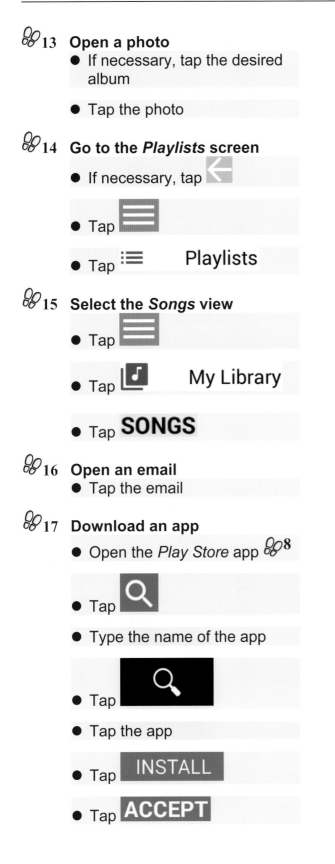

13 **Open a photo**
- If necessary, tap the desired album

- Tap the photo

14 **Go to the *Playlists* screen**
- If necessary, tap ⬅

- Tap ☰

- Tap ☷ Playlists

15 **Select the *Songs* view**
- Tap ☰

- Tap 🎵 My Library

- Tap **SONGS**

16 **Open an email**
- Tap the email

17 **Download an app**
- Open the *Play Store* app ⬚⬚**8**

- Tap 🔍

- Type the name of the app

- Tap 🔍

- Tap the app

- Tap INSTALL

- Tap ACCEPT

Appendix B. Index